ALL-CONSUMING
FIRE

OBJECT LESSONS FROM THE BOOK OF ACTS FOR KIDS

ANNE MARIE GOSNELL

All-Consuming Fire: Object Lessons from the Book of Acts for Kids

ISBN: 978-0-9981968-9-3 (print), 978-1-7351329-0-7 (epub)

Scripture quotations taken from the New American Standard Bible® (NASB), Copyright © 1960, 1962, 1963, 1968, 1971, 1972, 1973, 1975, 1977, 1995 by The Lockman Foundation. Used by permission. www.Lockman.org

ICB — Scripture taken from the International Children's Bible®. Copyright © 1986, 1988, 1999 by Thomas Nelson. Used by permission. All rights reserved.

Publishing and Design Services: MartinPublishingServices.com

"*All-Consuming Fire* is the latest addition to a collection of Bible-teaching books written by Anne Marie Gosnell. This book, like those before it, is a means to address the ongoing need for resources to more effectively communicate the Bible to children. It is not that children are not being taught the Bible, but rather that children's lives are not being transformed in the process. As I reviewed *All-Consuming Fire*, I was immediately aware that the key elements needed to reach the hearts of children are within every lesson. If you are looking for a way to ignite learning and change among your students, then you will find that this study of Acts is a means to that end."

—**MILTON V. UECKER ED.D.**; Professor Emeritus and former Dean; Columbia International University (CIU)

"Anne Marie Gosnell does it again in her 4th object lesson publication for kids. As always, Anne Marie has created another incredible resource guaranteed to make God's word come alive in the hearts and minds of children. Through engaging, creative methods, Anne takes children on an exciting journey through the book of Acts to God's all consuming fire. Definitely a must-have resource for both parents and teachers alike who are serious about effectively teaching solid biblical truths to children."

—**ESTHER MORENO**, Founder Child's Heart LLC

"I believe these are power packed lessons by Anne Marie. I love that she gives illustration and prop ideas so you can help kids really soak up these truths. Anytime you can help kids understand what you're talking about by showing them is a WIN!"

—**YANCY**, Songwriter, Producer & Worship Leader
YancyMinistries.com

"I am a huge fan of using illustrations to teach Biblical principles to kids and families. It was so encouraging to see Anne Marie pull together not only great illustrations but so many teaching supports for teachers of all experience levels. If you are new to teaching the Bible or are quite experienced and looking to increase your repertoire of biblical illustrations, this will be a great resource for you!"

—**JOSH DENHART**, KidMin Science + Lead Volunteers

"As always, Anne Marie delivers a powerful and practical book for those who teach the Bible! In this journey through the book of Acts, she doesn't shy away from deep truths or tough topics, but instead provides hands-on methods to make them come alive for kids! I highly recommend this book to anyone looking to teach their kids more about the Holy Spirit and the New Testament church."

—**JULIA BALL**, Owner of EquipFamily.com; Children's and Families Pastor, Newfoundland

DEDICATION

■ ■ ■ ■ ■ ■ ■ ■ ■ ■ ■ ■ ■ ■ ■ ■ ■ ■ ■

To my parents, Jim and Anne Hinson:

Thank you for taking me to church and serving in church ministry.
I met Jesus because you took me to church,
and I learned how to be in ministry by watching you.

I love you.

CONTENTS

FOREWORD

■ ■

George Barna, in his book on *"Transforming Children into Spiritual Champions"*, believes that children are changed through a deeper and lasting renovation of the heart. In 1970, Lawrence Richards, author of *Creative Bible Teaching,* addressed the same need when writing what today is still recognized as one of the most important works within the realm of Christian education. His influence is largely due to how his "hook, book, look, took" lesson outline offered a key to teaching that transforms. That book, written fifty years ago, is considered a classic because it remains the go to reference for those who desire that faith lessons are lived-out by students.

Teachers regularly spend time on a biblical passage or story (book) and questions to assess the degree to which the lesson is remembered or understood (look), but memorization and recall alone may only reach the head, and though important, does not change lives. However, it is the hook and the took elements of a lesson that reaches the heart. This is because gaining attention, creating motivation, and bridging to the student's life (emotion), must also be included within lessons if learning and more importantly knowing is the goal. Knowing from a biblical perspective is seeing the significance of truth and acting upon it, and what it means to "make disciples...teaching them to observe all that I have commanded." (Matthew 28: 19-20)

Lessons within *All Consuming Fire* are written and creatively designed to include the missing bookends that support biblical learning. Instruction begins by first gaining the students' attention and motivation (the hook), then teaching the Bible lesson (book and look), and concluding the lesson with the means to build (reflect) and then cross a bridge (obey) into the students' lives (the took). Each lesson offers teachers a well-constructed guide, that if followed, will include all the elements of effective instruction. Teachers simply need to add their own voice, style, pacing, and prayers for open hearts to each lesson and then watch expectantly as the Holy Spirit produces the fruit.

I trust that you will experience the joy that accompanies seeing children approach the Bible with enthusiasm and obediently design their means by which they will act upon the Truth. As you teach to transform lives you too will be transformed.

Milton V. Uecker Ed.D.
Professor Emeritus and former Dean
Columbia International University (CIU)

References referred to in this foreword:

- Richard, Lawrence & Bredfeldt, Gary J. *Creative Bible Teaching*. Revised and Expanded Edition. Chicago: Moody Press. 1970. 1998.
- Barna, George. *Transforming Children into Spiritual Champions*. Ventura, CA: Regal Books from Gospel Light. 2003.

INTRODUCTION

■ ■

Hey! I'm Anne Marie. Thank you for purchasing *All-Consuming Fire: Object Lessons from the Book of Acts for Kids.* This book includes 24 interactive object lessons for children ages 5 to 12. These weekly lessons are meant to last 20-30 minutes. I believe the title, *All-Consuming Fire*, correctly depicts God's idea of Holy Spirit living. God our Father loved us enough to send His Son to die for us so that we might live a Spirit-filled life. This life should consume every part of us.

This curriculum will help you:

- teach engaging Bible lessons children cannot resist;
- create a fun teaching atmosphere that sparks the imagination of children;
- teach children Biblical truth that enhances their spiritual growth; and
- share the gospel with children and expand the Kingdom.

I am humbled that you have chosen to use this resource! I pray that it will ignite a passion for Jesus in those who hear you teach.

For more resources for parents and teachers, visit futureflyingsaucers.com/consuming-fire-resource-page.

To receive weekly Bible lessons, book updates, and children's ministry helps, subscribe at futureflyingsaucers.com.

Keep on serving the Lord, my friend!

Anne Marie Gosnell
futureflyingsaucers.com

> Therefore, since we receive a kingdom which cannot be shaken, let us show gratitude, by which we may offer to God an acceptable service with reverence and awe; for our God is a consuming fire.
>
> —Hebrews 12:28-29

HOW THIS BOOK WORKS

███ ███ ███ ███ ███ ███ ███ ███ ███ ███ ███ ███ ███ ███

I have put these lessons in an order that encourages spiritual growth. However, the lessons do not have to be taught sequentially. These lessons can be taught with large groups or small groups. When planning your Bible lessons, whether at home or church, determine your objective first. Then look through the Table of Contents and decide which lessons will best help you reach your objective.

Each lesson has a **free downloadable poster** and other lesson helps that you can access from the **Resources Page** (futureflyingsaucers.com/consuming-fire-resource-page). Discuss and display the posters in the room throughout this series, and read them during each session. You may choose to use the shorter verses as memory verses.

Many lessons have a **Background** section. Use this section to help you put the lesson into context, or "set the stage," for the children.

New Testament history takes place in a variety of locations; therefore, there is a **Geography** section for each lesson. I encourage you to have a map to point out these places. See the Resources Page (https://www.futureflyingsaucers.com/consuming-fire-resource-page/) for maps.

The **Object Lesson** is usually first and might be referred to throughout the lesson. Most of the objects are items that many children know and see daily. Jesus used common objects such as sheep and trees when He taught, and we can do the same. Preparation time is minimal, and most lessons use materials you will find around your home. I do suggest practicing the lessons ahead of time to be sure you understand how the activity works.

The **Bible Lesson** section is a paraphrase of the event from the **Scripture Focus**. Read the Scripture to prepare for teaching your lesson. Afterward, read the Bible Lesson section a few times. Practice enough so that you can tell the story without reading.

The last section is essential: **Life Application**. This is where Scripture "comes alive" and the kids learn how to apply it to their lives. If we do not explain the purpose of Scripture to children, then you and I have failed as Bible teachers. All Scripture is useful, and we must showcase the glorious purpose of the Bible in each lesson.

At the end of each lesson is a **Comment Box**. This is an area for you to reflect upon your teaching so you can improve your skills. Thinking retrospectively will help you to evaluate your personal ministry. Ask yourself two questions: *"What went well as I taught this lesson?"* and *"What can I do better?"*

For more in-depth Bible teacher training, take a look at my online course, Become an Excellent Bible Teacher (futureflyingsaucers-bible-institute. teachable.com/p/excellent-bible-teacher).

I would love to know how your lessons go! Please share your retrospective ideas with me. Also, please leave a book review on the website of your favorite book store. Feel free to contact me at futureflyingsaucers@klopex.com. You can also join my Facebook group, Become an Excellent Bible Teacher: Bible Lessons for Kids (facebook.com/groups/BibleLessonsForKids).

A FEW LAST TIPS

■■■■■■■■■■■■■■■■■■■■■■■

Encourage the children to use their Bibles. Do not assume they think your story is Biblical just because you tell it. Have them be like the Bereans in the book of Acts. Show them in the Bible the verses you will be using. Some of the lessons will have the kids either reading along with you or reading for themselves. If you have children who do not read, you can still help them find the reference in the Bible. This is a great habit to start when young.

When you teach a lesson, try not to say words such as, *"Our story today comes from..."* While the Bible is the story of God, it is more than a story. We live in a world where the line between fairy tales, fiction, and truth is blurred. Because of this, refer to every person or event as history or biography. Children need to understand that people in Scripture were **real**, breathing people. The places in the Bible were—and some still are—**real** places.

Be enthusiastic when you teach. Do not put on a show, but share the joy of Jesus so that He is contagious! Scripture tells us that if Jesus is lifted up, He will draw all men to Him. Let us lift Him up!

One last thing...NEVER be afraid to share your testimony! Someone in the room might need to hear how God has worked in your past, how He is working today, and what He is doing in your future.

1 ON FIRE FOR JESUS

■ ■

Who is the Holy Spirit? Why should we care? Use this exciting Pentecost object lesson to teach children about the Holy Spirit and what happened when the disciples began to live a Spirit-filled life.

Scripture Focus: Acts 1-2

Materials:

- Two $10 bills (If you do not have US money, do not use plastic money.)
- Towel
- Lighter
- Rubbing alcohol
- Water
- Salt
- Glass bowl
- Metal tongs
- Fire extinguisher (just in case!)
- Acts 1:8 poster

**WARNING: This activity should not be done with children sitting close to you. Be sure you do not get your fingers wet.

Geography: Israel; Jerusalem

Background: After Jesus rose from the grave, He appeared to His followers over the duration of 40 days.

Preparation: Fill the glass bowl with 1/2 cup of rubbing alcohol, 1/2 cup of water, and 1/4 teaspoon of salt. Allow one of the $10 bills to soak in the bowl for at least 5 minutes while you talk.

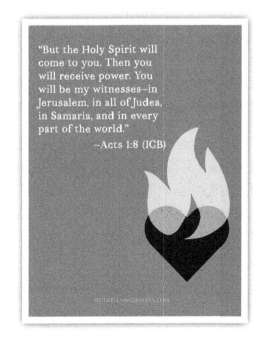

"But the Holy Spirit will come to you. Then you will receive power. You will be my witnesses—in Jerusalem, in all of Judea, in Samaria, and in every part of the world."
–Acts 1:8 (ICB)

FUTUREFLYINGSAUCERS.COM

OBJECT AND BIBLE LESSON

{Hold up one of the bills. Ask:}

> • This is valuable, isn't it? What would happen if I lit this $10 bill on fire? [It would burn.]

Let's say YOU are this $10 bill. You are valuable to God. He created you. He created me. But because of sin, we deserve death. The wages of sin is death.

BUT God sent Jesus, the Living Water, to save us from burning.

{Use the tongs to put the $10 bill in the clear liquid "water" in the bowl. Do NOT use your fingers! Read Acts 1:4-8.}

For 40 days after Jesus rose from the grave, He appeared off and on to the disciples. During that time He spoke to them about God and the kingdom of God.

The disciples were confused. They wondered when Jesus was going to restore the kingdom of Israel back to its former glory.

{Show the bowl with the money in it. Read Acts 1:9-17, 20-26.}

Like this $10 bill is soaking up the liquid, the disciples "soaked up" as much of the teaching of Jesus as they could. Knowledge, love, attitude, behaviors—ANYTHING they could soak up from Jesus, they did. Then one day, Jesus took them all up to the Mount of Olives. He told them to wait and receive the power of the Holy Spirit. Jesus explained that they were to be His witnesses throughout the world, and then He rose up into the air and left them.

Two angels told the disciples that Jesus would return one day the same way He had left. The disciples returned to Jerusalem. The 11 disciples were in the Upper Room, along with some women, Jesus' mother Mary, and Jesus' brothers. Judas Iscariot was no longer with the disciples, so they decided to choose another man to replace Judas.

{Ask:}

- Who was in the room waiting? [Peter, James, John, Andrew, Philip, Thomas, Bartholomew, Matthew, James, Simon, Judas son of James, Mary the mother of Jesus, Jesus' brothers, and some women]

- What were they doing in the room? [Praying]

- How many people were there? [About 120]

- What type of man would they choose to take the place of Judas Iscariot? [He had to have been with Jesus from the time John baptized Jesus until Jesus went up to heaven. He also had to be a witness of the Resurrection.]

- What does it mean to cast lots? [Casting lots was an Old Testament way of allowing God to show His answer, or will, for a decision. There is no mention of casting lots after Pentecost.]

Two men were chosen with these credentials: Justus and Matthias. Matthias received the position of being with the other 11 and was called an apostle.

And then the group of disciples waited.

{Read Acts 2:1-13.}

On the Day of Pentecost, the disciples were STILL gathered in the Upper Room. Pentecost was a Jewish festival, also called the Festival of Weeks, which was celebrated 50 days after the last day of the Passover. **(**Remember the Last Supper? That was during the Passover.)

Pentecost was originally a harvest festival, but over the years, the Jews began using this festival to celebrate the Law being given to Moses on Mt. Sinai. The Law had allowed Israel to become a nation as they traveled to take over their land and settle in it. The Law had allowed for the birth of a nation holy unto God.

{Ask:}

- On the Day of Pentecost, how were all of the disciples? [In one accord, or agreement, or one mind]

- What came from heaven? [A sound like rushing wind came from heaven and filled the room. Something like tongues of fire appeared to sit on them.]

- What happened next? [They were filled with the Holy Spirit and started to talk in different languages because the Holy Spirit gave them the power to do so.]

In Acts 2, something different happened on Pentecost. The 120 disciples were in the Upper Room when a sound of rushing wind came from heaven and filled the room. There appeared to be tongues of fire sitting on top of each disciple.

Each disciple had been with Jesus. They had soaked up, learned, and experienced the Living Water as much as they could.

{Show the bowl again. Use the tongs to pull out and hold the $10 bill over the bowl.}

As the tongues of fire were over the heads of the disciples, they started to speak in other languages.

{Use the lighter to light the $10 bill. The fire should burn off the alcohol and leave the bill solid, but wet. The water will not allow the bill the burn. The fire should flash quickly as it burns the alcohol.}

The Holy Spirit filled the disciples and, in a moment, they were gifted with the ability to speak other languages.

{Ask:}

- Who heard the disciples? [Jews, devout men, from every nation under heaven]
- What did they think about what they were hearing? [They were confused. They could each hear their own language being spoken, but they knew the people speaking were Galileans.]
- Why did they think the disciples were speaking this way? [The Jews thought the disciples were drunk with new wine.]

Because of the festival, Jews from the surrounding areas and countries were in Jerusalem. Evidently the rushing wind was REALLY loud because the Jews in Jerusalem gathered together in confusion. They were amazed to see poor Galileans speak in their own languages. Some were skeptical and stated that the disciples were drunk.

{Read Acts 2:14-15, 22-23, 37-42. Ask:}

- How did the people respond to Peter's words? [They were convicted of their sin (cut to the heart) and asked what they needed to do.]

Peter stood up and explained that they were not drunk; then he told the people all about the Scriptures and who Jesus was. He accused the people of killing Jesus, and they were cut to the heart! They asked what they needed to do. Peter told them to repent and be baptized. Three thousand souls were added to the church that day.

The church was born on Pentecost. The word *church* means a group of people who are separated out from a larger group. These believers in Jesus were a small group separated out from all of the other people. However, this small group was going to have more and more people added to it as the gospel was shared.

LIFE APPLICATION

■ ■

The Holy Spirit was sent by Jesus, God's Son. God is God. Jesus is God. The Holy Spirit is God. Each person of God has a purpose.

{Ask:}

- Remember the flame you saw? What happened to the bill first? [The bill had to be soaked in the liquid so the flame could burn without the bill burning up.]

When you accept the gift of eternal life through Jesus Christ, the Holy Spirit will come inside of you, or indwell, because you believe in Jesus. It doesn't hurt. Once the Spirit is there, you need to "soak" yourself by reading the Bible, going to church, praying, humbling yourself, seeking Jesus, and soaking up Jesus. Then you will be ready when the Holy Spirit wants to burn in your heart. He would love to tell you to do something, or teach you something new.

God is the All-Consuming Fire. He wants to burn in your heart so that you will have the same power and boldness that Peter had when he told those Jews about Jesus.

What can we learn from Pentecost? Unless you are soaked in Jesus, the fire of the Holy Spirit will not burn brightly. He might try to speak to you, correct you, and train you in the right things to do. If you are not soaked in Jesus, you might miss Him. Are you distracted? What do you need to do today so you are soaked in Jesus? Get soaked, and then watch the Holy Spirit burn in you as you tell others about Jesus!

COMMENT BOX

■ ■ ■ ■ ■ ■ ■ ■ ■ ■ ■ ■ ■ ■ ■ ■ ■ ■ ■ ■

THINK: What went well as you taught this lesson? What can you do better?

_____

_____

_____

_____

_____

_____

_____

_____

TIP: This is a dramatic Bible lesson! It will grab the attention of the children. Be sure to act as excited about it as they are!

2 THE EARLY CHURCH

■ ■

The tabernacle in the Old Testament was a picture of God dwelling with His people. In the New Testament, the Holy Spirit came to dwell within God's people. Use this lesson about the early church to teach children that the tabernacle was temporary, but the human temple is the home of the Holy Spirit.

Scripture Focus: Acts 2:1-7, 12-24, 37-39

Materials:

- Small tent (If you do not have a tent, use chairs, a large sheet, and clothes pins to make one.)
- Acts 2:38 poster

Geography: Jerusalem; Judea; Samaria; surrounding nations

Background: Jesus rose from the grave and appeared to many people. Then He ascended into heaven.

Peter said to them, "Change your hearts and lives and be baptized, each one of you, in the name of Jesus Christ for the forgiveness of your sins. And you will receive the gift of the Holy Spirit.

—Acts 2:38 (ICB)

FUTUREFLYINGSAUCERS.COM

If you know the facts of the gospel, then you will be able to tell someone the gospel when God gives you the opportunity. Choose to be knowledgeable:

1. We are sinners and deserve God's wrath because He is perfect and holy.

2. Jesus was born and lived on Earth.

3. Jesus died on the cross.

4. Jesus took our punishment and took God's wrath for us, separating Himself from His Father.

5. Jesus was buried in a tomb.

6. Jesus was resurrected from the dead.

7. If we have faith in Jesus, then we can have eternal life.

OBJECT LESSON

{Set up the tent. If you have a small number of children, have everyone enter the tent for the lesson. If you have a large number, place the tent so you can sit in the opening and have the children around you. Ask:}

- Have you ever been camping? [Allow for answers.]

- What did you like most about camping? [Allow for answers.]

- What did you like least about camping? [Allow for answers.]

- Have you ever traveled a long distance and camped along the way? [Allow for answers.]

- What did you miss most about your house when you finally came home? [Allow for answers.]

- What does the word dwelling mean? [Allow for answers; the word dwelling means to live, or to be with.]

Traveling in a tent can be fun for a while, but eventually you begin to miss having a home. If you live for a long time in a tent, it might rain and your things might get wet. Dirt or insects might get into the tent; wild animals might even try to get your food. A tent is not meant to be a permanent home. It is temporary.

We can dwell in a tent for a short while, but it is nice to have a permanent dwelling—one that does not blow away in the wind and rain.

BIBLE LESSON

Earlier during His ministry days, Jesus had changed Peter's name from Simon to Peter, which means *rock*. Jesus told Peter, *"Upon this rock I will build my church."*

Before Jesus ascended into heaven, Jesus and Peter had a deep conversation. Peter, who had denied Jesus three times, was asked if he loved Jesus. Three times Peter answered, *"You know, Lord, that I love you!"* Jesus asked Peter to feed His sheep.

{Read Acts 2:1-7, 12-24, 37-39.}

After Jesus' ascension, the disciples were huddled together in a room. Jesus had told them to go to Jerusalem and wait until He sent a Helper. One day, they heard the sound of rushing wind, and it filled the whole house. Then something like tongues of fire formed on top of the heads of each person in the room. All of the disciples began to speak in other languages that were not their native language.

The people in the street heard them and wondered how they heard their own language being spoken. Some of the people going past claimed that the men and women were drunk.

Peter, the man who had denied Jesus, stood up and began to preach the gospel. The people were "pierced to the heart" and asked what they needed to do. Peter told them to repent and be baptized. About 3,000 souls were added to the small group of believers.

{Ask:}

- In Peter's speech, what did he say would be poured out? [God's Spirit would be poured out on all flesh.]
- What happens to those who call on the name of the Lord? [They shall be saved.]
- Why do you think the disciples spoke in other languages? [It was the Passover. Many Jews from different countries were present. Speaking in the tongues of those Jews allowed them to hear the gospel in their own language.]

- Why do you think God would allow these disciples to speak in different languages? [Giving the disciples the power to speak other languages at this point in time allowed the gospel to be shared, acted upon, and then spread to other countries.]

Let's consider what God did in the Old Testament and what Jesus did in the Gospels:

- In the beginning, God came down and spoke.
- God walked and talked in the garden with Adam and Eve.
- God dwelt among His people, Israel, in the tabernacle. This was temporary.
- Jesus was born and spoke for Himself as the Son of God.
- Jesus walked and dwelt among men. This was temporary.
- The Holy Spirit came down and now teaches all things.
- The Holy Spirit dwells in our hearts if we believe and confess Jesus as our Lord. This is eternal!

The Old Testament, or Old Covenant, is over.

Jesus began a New Covenant.

All throughout the Old Testament, we read about God desiring to dwell with His people. He gave them directions to build the tabernacle, and He gave them the Law. Israel sinned. They could not follow the Law perfectly. They built a temple, a more permanent building, but they still could not keep God's Law.

When Jesus walked on the earth, Israel failed again. They failed to see Jesus as the Messiah. God still does what He chooses to do to save His people from themselves and from sin. With this plan, the Holy Spirit now guides us and dwells with us in our hearts.

Old Testament Covenant	God to Abraham	"I will make of you a great nation."	How God would bring salvation through the cross
New Testament Covenant	Jesus to Peter	"Upon you I will build my church."	How God would bring salvation to the Gentiles

LIFE APPLICATION

■ ■

The people who heard the gospel from the disciples were "cut to the quick," or their "hearts were pierced." This means they were convicted. When your spirit begins to be touched and changed by the Holy Spirit, you realize how sinful you are. You feel sorrow and sadness that you have disobeyed God.

{Ask:}

- How did the people respond to the gospel? [They asked, "What shall we do?"]

- What did Peter tell them? [Repent and be baptized.]

- What does the word repent mean? [If you are making a choice, you stop choosing wrong and choose something different. In this case, people were living without Jesus, dead in their sins; then they learned about Jesus, and they want Jesus to save them from their sin so they can live for Him.]

- What does verse 41 say happened? [There were people who gladly received Peter's words. They repented and were baptized. Three thousand people joined the church in one day.]

Have you ever had an experience like those 3,000 people? Have you ever told God you have repented? Have you ever desired to never sin again? If you are not sure, talk to God right now. You need to be sure. If you know that you have never repented, then I encourage you to do so.

{Lead the children in prayer. See the Extra Resources in the back of this book for tips for sharing the gospel with children.}

If you have believed in Jesus, then the same Holy Spirit who raised Jesus from the dead lives inside of you! It does not physically hurt when the Holy Spirit dwells in you.

You will still sin and fall into temptation; however, the Holy Spirit wants to guide you and teach you how to please God. He wants you to read the Bible and memorize Scripture so He can help you in times of need.

Going to church, learning the Bible, and memorizing Scripture are not a waste of time. The Holy Spirit will use whatever He can to help mold you into the image of Jesus.

What can we learn from the early church? When we are presented with truth and recognize that we have sinned, we should be sorry and agonize over that sin. We must understand that we need a Savior to save us from that sin. We need Jesus. When we place our faith in Jesus and surrender our lives to Him, then the Holy Spirit will dwell inside of us. This is good news!

COMMENT BOX

■ ■

THINK: What went well as you taught this lesson? What can you do better?

_____

_____

_____

_____

_____

_____

_____

_____

_____

_____

TIP: The fact of the Holy Spirit coming inside our hearts can be a strange idea to children. Some can become fearful. Reassure them that there is no pain. The Holy Spirit is spirit and not physical. This is a concept that will grow as children learn more about the Holy Spirit.

3 PETER, JOHN, AND A LAME MAN

████████████████████████████████████

Prayer is how we can communicate with God. There are times when we ask for something small, but God wants to bless us with something greater. Use this object lesson from Acts 3 to teach children about Peter, John, and the lame man.

Scripture Focus: Acts 3:1-10

Materials:

- 3 non-transparent cups (Label them 1, 2, and 3.)
- 3 different currency amounts (I used a quarter, a $1 bill, and a $20 bill. Make sure you have small, medium, and large currency values.)
- Acts 3:8 poster

{Preparation: Without the students watching, place the 3 cups upside down on a table. Under one, place the medium value currency. Under another one, place the greatest value currency. The third will remain empty. You will play a version of the game show *Let's Make a Deal*.}

Geography: Israel; Jerusalem

Background: On the day of Pentecost, the Holy Spirit swooped down onto the disciples in power, and over 3,000 people were added to the newly formed church.

But Peter said,
"I don't have any silver or gold,
but I do have something else I can give you:
By the power of Jesus Christ from Nazareth
—stand up and walk!"

—Acts 3:8 (ICB)

22

OBJECT LESSON

■ ■

{Give or show the students the lowest value currency.}

You, as a group, have this much money.

{Ask:}

- How much is that worth? [Allow for answer.]
- Would you like to have something better? Something that is worth more? [Yes]

I have three cups in front of me. You do not know what is under them. If you want to, you may choose whichever cup you would like, BUT you have to give me the money you already have. You lose it when you give it to me. You do not HAVE to choose a cup. You CAN keep the amount you have.

{If the group decides to choose a cup, take away the lowest value currency. Here are the options for what to say. Allow the students to continue "trading" until all of the cups have been turned over.}

Empty cup

{If chosen first, or after the lowest or greatest value cup} You exchanged your [least money amount] and received NOTHING! Oh, no! You took a risk, and unfortunately it did not turn out well for you.

Medium value cup

{If chosen first, or after the empty cup} This is better! Instead of [least money amount], now you have [medium money amount]! That is better. But is this the BEST that can happen?

{If chosen after the greatest value cup} Oh, no! You already had the BEST thing! And now you lost it. Well, [medium money amount] is better than nothing or [least money amount].

Greatest value cup

{If chosen first or second} WOW! [Greatest money amount]! That's better than [least money amount, middle money amount, or nothing]. I wonder if this is the best you can do? What else could be under these cups? Do you want to keep the [greatest money amount] or choose a new cup?

{If chosen as the last cup} WOW!! You now have the BEST! A [medium money amount] is better, but [greatest money amount] is best.

BIBLE LESSON

{Read Acts 3:1-10.}

After the day of Pentecost, Peter and John went to the temple to pray around 3:00 in the afternoon. At the same time, a lame man was being carried by some people and placed at his normal spot to beg for money, or alms. He was a poor man who had been lame from birth. The lame man saw Peter and John and asked for alms.

{Ask:}

- What does God want to do for us? Give us the best for us? Or not? [He wants to give us His best.]

The man called out for alms (money), and Peter replied that he had no silver or gold. How disappointing for the lame man! He needed money so he could eat and have a place to live. Imagine how disappointed he might have felt. He did not even have [lowest money amount] to exchange. He had nothing!

{Hold up the cup that had nothing under it.}

Peter continued, *"Silver and gold I do not have, but what I do have I will give to you. In the name of Jesus Christ, rise up and WALK!"* Peter grabbed the hand of the lame man and pulled him to his feet. The Bible says that strength came immediately to the lame man's feet!

{Hold up the middle value currency.}

The lame man wanted something better than what he had. He wanted money for his immediate needs. Peter could have given him a few coins, maybe enough for dinner that night, but then the man would have been begging again the next day.

{Hold up the greatest value currency.}

What Peter gave—what GOD gave—was something that was BEST! After being healed, the lame man could walk, fend for himself, get a job, and do everything any other person could do. The man was so overjoyed that he went walking and leaping and praising God all the way into the temple with Peter and John.

Everyone around knew who the lame man was and praised God with him. He had sat in that begging place for years, and now he was healed!

Peter noticed that all of the people were in awe, and he started to preach just as he had done on the day of Pentecost. He taught about the Old Testament, Jesus, and Jesus' death and resurrection from the dead.

LIFE APPLICATION

In the name of Jesus, Peter healed the lame man.

{Hold up the middle value currency.}

The lame man was seeking something better than what he had.

{Hold up the greatest value currency.}

God wanted to give the lame man what was best for him: healing.

There are times when we pray to God and ask Him for something that would improve our lives or the lives of people we love. Sometimes we seek a specific answer. Usually it's an answer we really want, such as a good grade on a test, a better friendship with someone, or a specific present at Christmas. Maybe you pray for your parents to stop fighting. Perhaps you want to be able to read better or work math problems better. Maybe someone is bothering you at school. Whatever it might be that you ask of God, it is good. It is good to ask. What if it isn't God's best for you? Should you pray differently?

What if you gave God your specific prayer request and asked Him to handle it His way? For example, maybe you have a friend who is really sick. That is a great request. Ask it. However, what if you said, *"Lord, please heal (name). But Lord, I want your best. I want Your will to be done. If there is anything else I can do to help my friend, please let me know"?*

{Talk through 2 or 3 more examples, helping the children to add the phrase, "Your will be done," or something similar to the prayer.}

This means we have to trust God with the understanding that He loves us and desires to do what is best for us. This also means that we might have to wait for an answer.

The lame man was healed immediately, but that does not mean God will answer our prayers immediately. He might. However, we can trust Him that He WILL answer.

Because of what God did, the man went walking and leaping and praising God.

{Ask:}

- What do you do when God blesses you and answers your prayer? Do you thank God for the good things in your life? [Allow for answers. What about your family? school? church? the nation you live in? your health? the fact that you CAN walk? What about thanking God for your weaknesses? That sounds crazy, doesn't it? Scripture tells us over and over that through the weakness of people, God is strong.]
- When you chose a different cup, you risked losing something. What did the lame man have to lose? [Allow for answers, but he probably had nothing to lose.]

When you swapped cups, you took a risk. It was risky to trade the [least money amount] and [medium money amount]. It was not so risky if you had nothing.

Serving God seems risky. In reality, everything we have belongs to God. We do not know what He is going to do when we come to Him with our prayers. We CAN trust Him completely. When we surrender to God, we are telling Him that He is totally in charge.

God is the only One who is completely faithful. Sometimes because of our own sinful choices, we come to God with nothing. All we can do is offer ourselves... and that is what He wants. Everything!

What can we learn from Peter, John, and the lame man? Sometimes we hold out our prayers and ask for something little when God has something much bigger and better in mind for us. We must be willing to give everything to the One who is absolutely trustworthy!

COMMENT BOX

■ ■

THINK: What went well as you taught this lesson? What can you do better?

_____

_____

_____

_____

_____

_____

_____

_____

TIP: This lesson can cause some serious discussion about why God sometimes chooses to heal and other times chooses not to heal. It is OK to let children know that we do not understand everything that God does. His ways are not like ours, but He is totally good and completely faithful.

4 ANANIAS AND SAPPHIRA

Satan is known as the deceiver. Sin can look good, even beautiful, at times, but it is deceptive. Use images of three deceptive animals to teach this object lesson about Ananias and Sapphira.

Scripture Focus: Acts 5:1-11

Materials:

- Pictures of cute or beautiful animals that are deadly (I used the blue ring octopus, the poison dart frog, and the platypus. See the Resources Page.)
- Acts 5:11 poster

Geography: Israel; Jerusalem

Background: After the day of Pentecost, people continued to join the disciples and follow Jesus. People were meeting and eating together. Some were being healed. Some were selling everything they had to give the money to the disciples. People were being changed from the inside out.

The whole church and all the others who heard about these things were filled with **FEAR.**

–Acts 5:11 (ICB)

FUTUREFLYINGSAUCERS.COM

OBJECT LESSON

■ ■ ■ ■ ■ ■ ■ ■ ■ ■ ■ ■ ■ ■ ■ ■ ■ ■ ■

I love animals! Some are really large. Others are tiny. Some are colorful, while others are drab. I have some animals for us to discuss. I am going to hold up a picture, and let's see what makes them special.

{Hold up the frog image. Ask:}

- What makes this animal special? [Allow for answers. Have them discuss description, movement, food, location...whatever they might know about this type of frog. Ask if anyone knows what this frog is called. This is a poison dart frog. One frog has enough poison to kill 10 to 20 men. In fact, tribal peoples in the rain forest used to use poison dart frogs on their spears.]

{Hold up the octopus image. Ask:}

- What makes this animal special? [Allow for answers. Have them discuss description, movement, food, location...whatever they might know about this type of octopus. Ask if anyone knows the name of this octopus. This is a blue ring octopus. They are small and beautiful, but they have enough poison to kill a man.]

{Hold up the platypus image. Ask:}

- What makes this animal special? [Allow for answers. Have them discuss description, movement, food, location...whatever they might know about the platypus. Be sure to discuss how cute and fuzzy they are. Then explain that the platypus has poisonous ankle spurs, and while they will not kill a man, they sure can hurt a person.]

These animals are deceptive. The frog is shiny and beautiful. So is the octopus. And the platypus looks so fun and fuzzy! They do not look dangerous, but they are. Sin can be that way. It looks good, even beautiful, but it can be deadly. The wages of sin is death.

BIBLE LESSON

{Tell the story or read Acts 5:1-11.}

After the lame man was cured, Peter and John were arrested for preaching in the name of Jesus. The high priest told them to stop preaching, but Peter and John told him that they could not stop telling people about all the things they had seen and heard.

{Ask:}

- Who else behaved this way after meeting Jesus? [The shepherds at Jesus' birth, people whom Jesus healed, etc.]

When people meet Jesus and know who He is, they cannot help but be changed. However, sometimes there are those who meet Jesus and do not change because they do not understand who He is.

The people's hearts were changed by their faith in Jesus. They started to bring the disciples money and items to give to those who might not have anything. Barnabas was one of these people. He sold some land and brought all of the money to the feet of the disciples (Acts 4:36-37). However, not everyone was as generous.

Ananias and his wife were not as generous. There were some things about God they did not understand. When we deal with God, we need to understand who God is. This is why reading and knowing your Bible is so important. This is how you learn about God. God is not deadly and dangerous, but He is holy, perfect, and just.

Ananias and Sapphira sold some of their land. They plotted together to keep some of the money for themselves, but *claim* that they were bringing ALL of the money to the disciples. This was deceitful!

{Ask:}

- Were they required to sell the land? [No]
- Were they required to give any money? [No. Yet they chose to lie.)

Ananias came first, brought the money, and told Peter he had sold the land for a certain amount. Peter, being full of the Holy Spirit, asked Ananias why he would lie to the Holy Spirit. Why lie to God? Ananias dropped dead. Some men came in, picked up his body, and buried it outside.

Three hours later, Sapphira came into the room, not knowing what had happened to her husband. Peter asked, *"Is this the amount for which you sold the land?"* She answered, *"Yes."* She died immediately. The same men who buried her husband carried her out and buried her.

Peter gave her an opportunity to tell the truth, but she did not. God takes sin seriously. He will not be mocked.

LIFE APPLICATION

The Bible tells us that, after the deaths of Ananias and his wife, a great fear spread throughout the early believers. This fear was filled with awe, knowing that God is the One who causes life and death. God is the One in charge of everything.

We must not think that we can sin and not receive the consequences of the sin. We must choose to obey God and His ways instead. After all, His ways are best for us.

{Hold up the pictures of the animals.}

These animals seem harmless. However, once you really know about them, you realize that you do not want to encounter one of these.

There are choices and situations that might seem harmless at first, but if you educate yourself about those things, you will realize that you should run from them.

{Choose and discuss a few age-appropriate examples. See below:}

Preschool Example: Getting mad and throwing a temper tantrum when you do not get your way or when you lose a game is a bad habit to start. It might seem harmless, but if you choose to do these things, you hurt your relationships with other people. You might not have friends who want to play with you. What should you do instead?

Elementary Example: Taking something that does not belong to you is a bad habit to start. You might take something from your parents first, and then try to take a candy bar from a store. Then it might grow into shoplifting and eventually burglary. You could end up in jail. Something so small and seemingly innocent can grow to be a life-changing choice. What should you do if you desire something that is not yours?

Upper Elementary/Middle School Example: Drugs, food, smoking, alcohol, and pornography can become addictive substances. One joint, one beer, one cigarette or vape, or one look at a website might seem like nothing. But your choices with these things can ruin your relationships with people you love. You could become drunk. You could drive under the influence of alcohol, crash the car, and kill someone. You could choose to steal because you need your next fix of drugs or alcohol. If you mess with porn, then you will mess up your relationship with your future spouse. Choosing to smoke, or to eat too much or too little, does not take care of your body where the Holy Spirit dwells if you are saved. Choose today how you will handle these things. Ask the Holy Spirit to help you be wise. Do not be deceived.

Sin is deceptive. People can be deceptive. If you are not careful, you could lie and deceive just like Ananias and Sapphira. If you believe in Jesus, then you have the Holy Spirit living inside of you. He is the One who gives you the power to run away from sinful choices.

It is important to understand why God takes sin so seriously. Sin and selfishness ruin families, marriages, friendships, and relationships of all kinds. We serve a God who is all about relationships. HE is trustworthy. If we bear the name *Christian*, then we must be trustworthy as well.

What can we learn from Ananias and Sapphira? God is holy and just. He wants a good relationship with those He created. That means sin must be dealt with. God loves us so much that He sent Jesus to take our sin upon Himself. He died because of your sin. In return, we should obey God and live a life that shows God that we love Him and other people.

COMMENT BOX

THINK: What went well as you taught this lesson? What can you do better?

_____

_____

_____

_____

_____

_____

_____

_____

TIP: Use this lesson to talk candidly about certain sins. If the church does not teach children God's truth, then the world will teach them its truth.

5 APOSTLES ON TRIAL

■ ■

When life is good, it is easy to thank God for blessings. What about during times of suffering? Did you know that suffering has a purpose? Use this object lesson about the apostles and suffering to teach children that thanksgiving through suffering produces the assurance of salvation.

Scripture Focus: Acts 5:12-42

Materials:

- 3-4 tea light candles (number depends on the size of the vase or jar)
- Glass vase or jar with an opening large enough to fit 3-4 candles
- Large glass baking pan
- Water
- Lighter or matches
- Acts 5:41 poster

Geography: Israel; Jerusalem

Background: The Holy Spirit descended upon the disciples in the Upper Room. More and more people joined the new church. Miracles and preaching caused an uproar in Jerusalem.

The apostles
left the meeting
FULL OF JOY
because they were
given the honor of
suffering disgrace for Jesus.

—Acts 5:41 (ICB)

FUTUREFLYINGSAUCERS.COM

OBJECT LESSON

{Place the 3-4 tea lights in the middle of the glass baking pan. Light the candles.}

When Jesus was on Earth, He told people that His disciples are to be like lights on a hill in a dark world.

{Ask:}

- How can you be a light to other people? [Allow for answers.]

The apostles were those in the early church who spread the teachings of Jesus, mainly the twelve disciples and Paul. Even today, if you share the gospel and teach others about Jesus, then, by general definition, you are an apostle. However, we usually use the terms *disciple* or *missionary* in churches today.

BIBLE LESSON

{Tell the story or read Acts 5:12-32.}

The apostles of the early church experienced power like they had never known. The church was of one mind and one spirit, and amazing things happened! More and more people came to know Jesus. The people were so amazed by what they saw, that they brought the sick out to the streets just so the shadow of Peter might fall upon them. Every day the apostles went to the temple, at Solomon's Porch, where the lame man had been healed, to preach about Jesus.

The high priest was not happy. He led the Sadducees, and they arrested the apostles and put them in prison. (Remember, the Sadducees did not believe in the resurrection or in angels.)

That night, an angel of the Lord came to the prison cell, opened the doors, and brought them out. The angel told them to go back into the temple and preach.

The apostles obeyed and went back to the temple in the morning to teach.

{Ask:}

- Do we know which apostles were put in jail? [No, Scripture does not tell us, but because it uses plural pronouns, we can determine that it was more than one.]
- What did the high priest find the next day? [The guards went to get the prisoners only to find that they were not there. The guards were outside the doors, but no prisoners were inside!]

The high priest and the others of the council did not know what to do. While they wondered, a person came up to them and exclaimed that the prisoners were all teaching in the temple again.

{Ask:}

- In whose name did the high priest not want them to teach? [Jesus']

• How did Peter respond? [Peter replied, "We ought to obey God rather than man. We are Jesus' witnesses and we have also been given the Holy Spirit because we obey Him."]

The Jewish council was furious, and they plotted the death of the apostles. Then a wise Pharisee named Gamaliel stood up and spoke to the group. He said, *"If this movement is of man, it will fail and disappear. If it is of God, you cannot overthrow it, because you would be fighting against God."*

The council agreed. They beat the disciples, commanded them to stop teaching in Jesus' name, and let them go.

Peter and John rejoiced as they left the temple. They were thankful to suffer for Jesus. The next day they returned to the temple to preach and teach in Jesus' name. They were being lights on a hill.

LIFE APPLICATION

■ ■

Suffering with an attitude of thanksgiving—that sounds a little crazy to us. These apostles were beaten and scolded, and people plotted their deaths. Yet they rejoiced because they suffered in honor of Jesus. They were thankful to be used by God.

Look at the lights in this pan. They are glowing and seem so happy!

But when bad times come, or we suffer for the name of Jesus, it is hard to be joyful and let our lights shine like the apostles did.

{Pour water into the glass baking pan until the water line is almost to the top of the tea light candles. They should not float. Turn the glass vase upside down and place it over all of the candles. The fire should go out, and water should be sucked into the vase, allowing the tea lights to rise on the water.}

Suffering is a strange thing. We share our lights every day when things are going well. However, when suffering comes along, it seems that our lights go out, like these candles.

{Ask:}

- What happened when the apostles were placed in jail? [An angel opened the prison doors and brought them out.]
- What happened to the candles when I placed the vase over them? [The lights went out.]
- How do you think the apostles felt after being released by the angel? [Allow for answers.]
- What happened the next day? [The guards went to get the apostles, but they were not in the prison; they were preaching in the temple.]
- How do you think the apostles felt when they were arrested again? [Allow for answers; they may have felt frightened, nervous, scared, or frustrated.]

When the apostles were thrown in jail, I wonder if they thought their lights had gone out. They could not tell many people about Jesus while sitting in a jail cell. When they were released a second time, the apostles were beaten and told they could not preach about Jesus any more.

{Ask:}

- How did the apostles respond to the high priest? [They told the high priest that they had to obey God and not man.]
- After the apostles were beaten, what did they do? [They rejoiced and continued preaching.]
- After these lights went out, what happened? [The water was sucked into the vase, and the candles rose.]

Even though the lights of our candles went out, they rose up in the air. The water was under them, pushing them up.

The apostles suffered in jail and were beaten, but they responded with rejoicing and thanksgiving. Jesus was with those apostles through all of that suffering. Jesus, who is the Living Water, was there to lift them up and encourage them even when their light was dim or out.

In many nations, people do not really know what it is like to suffer, or be persecuted, for believing in Jesus. But there are people in other countries who are not allowed to have Bibles; they cannot claim to be a Christian or go to church. If they do, they could be arrested, put in jail, and possibly killed.

The Bible tells us that our salvation is perfected through suffering (Hebrews 2:10). We are also told to rejoice in our suffering because God uses it to strengthen our character, or who we are (Romans 5:3-4). Christians are supposed to offer sacrifices of praise and thanksgiving (Psalm 107:22, 116:17).

{Ask:}

- What is sacrifice? [The giving up of something]

The apostles, through their beatings and afflictions, were not only sacrificing their physical bodies. They were also sacrificing who they were as people, such as their families, livelihoods, property, etc.

They were telling the Jewish council that Jesus and His message of salvation were more important than their lives. What was the worst thing the Jewish council could do? Kill them? That would allow the apostles to enter heaven and eternal glory. That is a Christian's hope. There is no sadness in that.

Jonah 2:9 tells us: *"I will sacrifice to You with a voice of thanksgiving. I will fulfill what I have vowed. Salvation is from the Lord!"*

What can we learn from the apostles on trial? We can be thankful and joyful when we suffer in life because God uses hard times to teach us more about who He is. He teaches us to rely upon Him and not ourselves. He teaches us how to pray during hard times as well. Through suffering, God teaches us that we must depend upon Him to lift us up. God wants a relationship with us.

COMMENT BOX

■ ■

THINK: What went well as you taught this lesson? What can you do better?

_____

_____

_____

_____

_____

_____

_____

_____

_____

TIP: This science experiment might be difficult for a large group to see. Consider having the children gather around you, or having smaller groups come to you for the lesson.

6 THE STONING OF STEPHEN

■■■■■■■■■■■■■■■■■■■■■■■■■■■

How do you want your life to end? Use this object lesson about the stoning of Stephen to discuss how life is like a race and how focusing on Jesus and being filled with the Holy Spirit helps one run a good race.

Scripture Focus: Acts 6-7

Materials:

- White board or chalk board (if you create the chart)
- Trophy, ribbon, or some other major award
- Acts 7: 55-56 poster

Geography: Israel; Jerusalem

Background: The Holy Spirit descended upon the disciples in the Upper Room. Miracles and preaching caused an uproar in Jerusalem. The apostles were persecuted, but they responded with thanksgiving. More and more people were joining the early church each day.

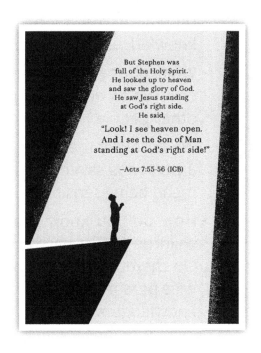

But Stephen was full of the Holy Spirit. He looked up to heaven and saw the glory of God. He saw Jesus standing at God's right side. He said,

"Look! I see heaven open. And I see the Son of Man standing at God's right side!"

–Acts 7:55-56 (ICB)

OBJECT AND BIBLE LESSON

{This is a great Bible event with which you can create a comparison and contrast list. Keep it simple for young children. Show the trophy and ask:}

- Have you ever won an award? [Allow for answers.]
- What did you have to do to earn the award? [Allow for answers. Hopefully answers will include terms such as: train hard, work hard, study a lot, persevere, etc.]

{Read Acts 6:1-8.}

After the apostles were persecuted, the church continued to grow and grow and grow! Because there were so many people, a complaint was made by a group of Greek Jews. They claimed that their widows were being neglected by the apostles. The twelve men did not want anyone overlooked. They gathered everyone together and said, "*Choose seven men among you so that they might do this business.*" The apostles needed to teach and pray. The apostles could not possibly serve every need. Others could do that.

{Ask:}

- What type of men were to be chosen? [They were to have a good reputation, be full of the Holy Spirit, and wise. (Wisdom means using knowledge, experience, and good judgment to make decisions.)]
- What does having a good reputation mean? [Allow for answers. Guide children to describe a person of good reputation as well thought of by other people.]
- What does it mean to be full of the Holy Spirit? [Allow for answers. Once a person is saved, the Holy Spirit dwells inside of him or her. It can also mean being sensitive to the Spirit and having a desire to follow the Spirit.]
- How do you know if a person is wise? [Allow for answers. Explain to children that a person can know a lot of information and not be wise. On the other hand, a person can be less intelligent and be very wise. A wise person is someone who, through life experiences, knows how to use knowledge well.]

Seven men, or deacons, were chosen. One was Stephen. The Scriptures say he was full of faith, the Holy Spirit, and power. He also did wonders and signs among the people.

Then a group of people started to argue with Stephen.

{On the board write "Enemies" and "Stephen." This story is filled with action! As you tell the story or read the Scripture, write down the verbs describing the actions of each. Read Acts 6:8-15; then go to Acts 7:54-60.}

BEFORE STEPHEN'S SERMON	
ENEMIES	**STEPHEN**
Argued with him Persuaded others Stirred up people Seized him Brought him to the council Set up false witnesses	Spoke with wisdom Full of the Holy Spirit
AFTER STEPHEN'S SERMON	
Cut to the heart Gnashed teeth Cried out Stopped their ears Cast him out Put cloaks at the feet of Saul Stoned him	Gazed into heaven Saw the glory of God and Jesus Called on God Forgave his enemies

These enemies of Stephen were so angry! They couldn't seem to win against Stephen when he spoke and preached about Jesus.

{Ask:}

- Why could they not win against Stephen? [He was filled with the Holy Spirit. Stephen preached in such a way that the council could not win.]
- What do you notice about the enemies? [Allow for answers.]
- What do you notice about Stephen? [Allow for answers.]

Picture this: The mob grabbed Stephen and dragged him outside the city. He was thrown down, and the people surrounded him. They picked up rocks and threw them at Stephen. Stephen lifted his head up to heaven and saw Jesus **standing** beside the Father.

This is significant! Nowhere else in Scripture are we told of Jesus **standing** beside the Father. Usually He is sitting beside the Father.

{Ask:}

- Why is it that when Stephen saw Jesus, He was standing? [Allow for answers.]

LIFE APPLICATION

{Show the trophy and ask:}

- Have you ever been to a race or watched one on TV? What are the spectators, those watching, doing? [Standing and jumping and yelling for the racers]
- When you earned your trophy or award, what did the audience do? [Allow for answers. The audience probably applauded.]

The Bible tells us that every Christian is running a "race," a race of life. We want to run our race in such a way that it pleases Jesus.

We are not told why Jesus was standing, but perhaps Jesus was standing for Stephen. Maybe Jesus was pleased with Stephen and the way he ran his race. However, Jesus would not have been pleased that one of His children was being harmed. The stoning continued, and Stephen forgave his enemies. He closed his eyes...and then he was with Jesus. He probably heard the words, *"Well done, good and faithful servant!"*

Stephen was the first martyr, or person to die for his faith in Jesus. There have been many, many more martyrs through the years, including people today who are killed because they believe in Jesus.

What can we learn from the stoning of Stephen? Life is an adventure. It is a race. It is not a race that we compete with others to win; it is a race that we train for and persevere through, and someday we will cross the finish line of death into heaven. How will you choose to run your race? Like Stephen? Jesus will be with you every step of the way.

COMMENT BOX

■ ■ ■ ■ ■ ■ ■ ■ ■ ■ ■ ■ ■ ■ ■ ■ ■ ■ ■

THINK: What went well as you taught this lesson? What can you do better?

_____

_____

_____

_____

_____

_____

_____

_____

_____

TIP: When you are telling this story, be dramatic about the stoning. When you get to the part about Jesus standing, if you are sitting, stand up. You might want to applaud. Bringing out emotion helps children remember Biblical ideas.

7 A SORCERER AND AN ETHIOPIAN

■■■■■■■■■■■■■■■■■■■■■■■■

Can we be sure that we are saved from our sins? Use this Bible lesson about a sorcerer and an Ethiopian to explore the idea of experiencing God and total heart change.

Scripture Focus: Acts 8 (This is a lot of Scripture. You can either narrate the events or have older children read the Scripture sections.)

Materials (choose 3-4 pairs of products):

- Vanilla frosting and shortening
- Milk and buttermilk
- Sugar and salt
- Paprika and chili powder
- Whipped cream and shaving cream
- Baking soda and confectioner's sugar
- Ketchup and hot sauce
- Spoons or containers for chosen pairs of food
- Cookie sheet
- Volunteer(s)
- Acts 8:37 poster

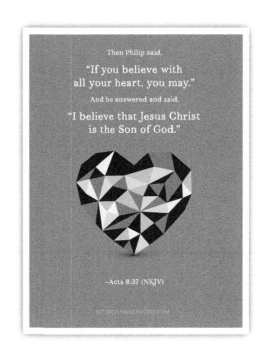

{Preparation: Put a taste of each food on a spoon. Set up the spoon pairs on a cookie sheet. Do not allow the children to see you setting this up. Try to make the matching foods look exactly the same on the spoons.}

Geography: Israel; Jerusalem; Samaria; Gaza

Background: More and more people were joining the early church each day. Because there were so many people, seven men, or deacons, were chosen to serve the people. One of those chosen was Stephen, the first martyr of the church.

OBJECT LESSON

{Choose a volunteer(s) who will handle the taste-testing with a fun attitude. You could use a volunteer for each food pair. Lead them to taste the "bad" version first. Say:}

We are going to do a taste test. I am going to give you a food to try, and I am going to tell you what I think it is. You tell me if I am correct or not.

{Give the spoonful of shortening. Ask:}

- I think this is frosting. Yes? [No; allow for sputtering and reactions.]

{Give the spoonful of frosting. Ask:}

- Is this the frosting? [Yes!]

{Continue with the other 2-3 foods you chose. Say:}

These food pairs looked a lot alike. The only way to really know what they were was to taste them. We will come back to this in a minute.

BIBLE LESSON

{Read Acts 8:1-8.}

When Stephen was stoned, those who were throwing the rocks laid their cloaks at the feet of a young man named Saul. He agreed with the stoning. He was a Pharisee. He loved God and God's Law. He knew that these people who followed Jesus were wrong and were causing trouble. Therefore, he went after them.

{Ask:}

- Picture a cow walking into a store that sells a lot of glass items. What would happen? [Everything would break! Glass would go everywhere.]

That is what happened when Saul went after the people of the early church. Everyone scattered. He arrested men, women, and children, and even had people put to death. Persecution of the early church began with the death of Stephen. Christians fled from Jerusalem. They went to Judea, Samaria, and even farther lands.

Another deacon was named Philip. Like Stephen, he was a man of good reputation, wise, and full of the Holy Spirit. He is known as Philip the Evangelist. All people who love Jesus are told to help spread the gospel, but sometimes God chooses specific people to totally dedicate their lives to preaching Jesus to other people. And that is what Philip did.

{Read Acts 8:9-25.}

Philip went to Samaria and preached Jesus to the people. There was a man named Simon the Sorcerer who had made himself great in the community by practicing sorcery. All the people said that he had great power. Philip started preaching, and people started to believe in Jesus. Lives were being changed, and people were being baptized. Simon followed Philip, amazed at all of the miracles and wonders that happened through Philip. Simon decided to believe in Jesus and be baptized as well.

For some reason the Holy Spirit had not come to these new Christians after they had been baptized. Peter and John went to Samaria. When they laid their hands on the people, the Holy Spirit filled the people. Simon watched this and exclaimed to Peter, *"I want the power to do that! How much can I pay you?"*

Peter looked at him and rebuked him! He told Simon that a gift of God cannot be purchased with money. Peter explained that Simon was full of bitterness and sin, that he needed to repent, and that maybe he could be forgiven. Simon asked Peter to pray for him so that the things Peter said would not happen.

{Read Acts 8:26-40.}

Meanwhile, an angel appeared to Philip and told him to travel to Gaza. He obeyed right away and without question. In the distance he saw a chariot. The Holy Spirit told Philip to go and catch up to the chariot. When Philip was close, he heard the man reading from the Old Testament book of Isaiah.

The man in the chariot is called the Ethiopian eunuch in Scripture, but he probably was from the nation of Nubia just below Egypt, and not from Ethiopia. The Greeks would use the term *Ethiopian* for all black-skinned people. This man was the treasurer for Queen Candace. *Candace* was a title (similar to the title *Pharaoh* in Egypt), not the name of the queen. This man was a high government official in his country, and he worshipped Yahweh (God).

Philip asked the man, *"Do you understand what you are reading?"* This man who was great in his country and rich in influence said, *"How can I? I need someone to help me."* Philip joined him in the chariot and proceeded to preach Jesus to this man. They drove past some water, and the man asked if he could be baptized. *"If you believe in Jesus with all your heart,"* Philip replied.

The Ethiopian eunuch was baptized, and afterward the Spirit caught Philip up. Philip appeared in a town about 20 miles north of Gaza.

As for the Ethiopian, he rejoiced and returned to his country.

LIFE APPLICATION

Let's think about what was the **same** for Simon the Sorcerer and the Ethiopian. Both had heard Philip preach the gospel. Both had said they believed in Jesus. Both were baptized.

The food we had looked the same on the outside. Both Simon and the Ethiopian had done the same things.

Once the food was tasted, you could tell something wasn't right.

{Ask:}

- What was different about Simon and the Ethiopian? [Allow for answers.]
- What did Peter say was wrong with Simon? [He thought the gift of the Holy Spirit could be purchased; His heart was not right with God; He was poisoned by bitterness and sin.]

Simon: Before Philip came, Simon claimed that he was great when he was not. He practiced sorcery and trickery to get the people to listen to him. Even though Simon *said* he believed in Jesus, he did not have the Holy Spirit in him, and he wanted to pay Peter for God's power. Therefore, Simon did not believe in Jesus with his whole heart. The Scriptures tell us that even the demons believe in Jesus and are fearful of Him.

This Scripture shows us that people can say words, say a prayer, answer all the questions correctly, be baptized, and STILL not have a changed, humble, repentant heart for Jesus.

Ethiopian: He was great in his country, but humble because he knew he did not understand what he was reading. He asked for help and God supplied it through Philip.

The Ethiopian shows us what salvation and repentance look like. He humbled himself so he could know God's truth, and he confessed about Jesus by saying, *"I believe that Jesus Christ is the Son of God."* After he was baptized, he left rejoicing. As a result, it might be because of this one man and his influence that the Christian church began in Africa.

{Ask:}

- How did you know that the foods were not what I said they were? [Because they were tasted]

You had to experience the foods to find out if they were what they were supposed to be.

{Ask:}

- How do you know if you are saved? [A saved person confesses that Jesus is their Lord; they experience Jesus, are guided by the Holy Spirit, and experience a changed heart and a changed perception about the world.]
- What do you think the verse, *"Taste and see that the Lord is good,"* means? [Allow for answers.]
- Do we actually eat God? [No]
- How do we fill ourselves with God? [Once we are saved, the Holy Spirit dwells in us. We must keep on being filled with God's Word.]
- How can we stay in community with Jesus? [Through prayer and going to church with other believers]

Sin is everything you think, say, and do that is not pleasing to God. You sin and fall short of what God wants from you. Therefore, God sent Jesus. Jesus died instead of you according to the Scriptures. If you believe with your whole heart that Jesus died on the cross, came back to life after three days, and is now in heaven with God, that is a start. You also need to confess that Jesus is your Lord, which means He is in charge of your life. When you know Jesus saved you from your sins, then with a humble heart you should want to surrender everything you have to Him. Then the Holy Spirit will come and dwell inside of you to guide you to follow the commands of Jesus.

What can we learn from a sorcerer and an Ethiopian? Words do not save you. Being baptized does not save you. Only faith, or trusting in Jesus with your whole heart, will save you from sin and death.

COMMENT BOX

████████████████████████████████

THINK: What went well as you taught this lesson? What can you do better?

_____

_____

_____

_____

_____

_____

_____

_____

_____

TIP: Because some of the foods on the spoons taste bad, you might want to have a trash can or sink nearby. You might want a camera, too. You are bound to have some funny faces! (Be sure to ask permission before taking pictures.)

8 THE CONVERSION OF SAUL

■■■■■■■■■■■■■■■■■■■■■■■■

What happens when a person encounters Jesus? Use this Bible lesson on the conversion of Paul to discuss being empty vessels and how we can be instruments for God.

Scripture Focus: Acts 9

Materials:

- Vase or empty container
- Volunteers to act out the story event
- Acts 9:4 poster

Geography: Israel; Jerusalem; Damascus

Background: Persecution of the early church had begun with the death of Stephen. The Christians fled from Jerusalem. They went to Judea, Samaria, and even farther lands. Philip went to Samaria and preached Jesus to the people. There he encountered the sorcerer, and then he was led to meet an Ethiopian.

FUTUREFLYINGSAUCERS.COM

And falling to the ground, he heard a voice saying to him,

"Saul, Saul, why are you persecuting me?"

—Acts 9:4 (ESV)

OBJECT LESSON

{Show the vase to the children. Ask:}

- What is a vessel? [A container that is empty that can be filled]

- What can we put in here? [Allow for answers, such as water, flowers, etc.]

- Do you remember at whose feet the cloaks were cast when Stephen was stoned? [Saul's]

This is an empty vessel. A vessel can also be called an *instrument*—not a musical instrument, but a tool that can be useful. God considers us to be vessels, or instruments, and Saul is a great example of one for us.

BIBLE LESSON

In Acts 8, we learned that Saul was trying to destroy the church. Scripture tells us that he "breathed" threats and murder against the church. He went to the high priest and asked for permission to go to Damascus to arrest those of The Way. Papers were granted, and Saul and some other men set off.

{Read Acts 9: 1-25. Choose volunteers to act for Paul, a few men traveling with Paul, Jesus, and Ananias as you read. If you have enough children, have a small group be angry Jews and another group be disciples. Have Saul walk along the road using angry body language. Have Jesus use questioning gestures. Encourage Ananias to be scared as Jesus talks to him and to be confident when he meets Saul.}

When Saul was almost to Damascus, a blinding light from heaven caused him to fall to the ground. A voice said, *"Saul, why are you persecuting me?"* Saul asked who was speaking to him, and the voice answered, *"Jesus."* Saul asked Jesus what He wanted him to do. Jesus told Saul to go into Damascus, and there he would be told what to do. When the light was gone, Saul was blind. The men around him had heard the voice, but had seen no one. The men led Saul into the city.

Ananias was a man of The Way who was in Damascus. The Lord spoke to him in a dream. Jesus told him to go to a street called Straight, where he would find Saul of Tarsus. He told Ananias that Saul would have a vision of a man named Ananias who would come to him and give him back his sight.

Ananias had heard about Saul. Ananias told God that Saul had the authority to harm the saints. The Lord replied, *"Go, for he is a chosen vessel of Mine, to bear My name before the Gentiles, kings, and the children of Israel."* Ananias obeyed and went to Saul. He found Saul in a house, laid his hands on him, and said, *"Brother Saul, Jesus has sent me to you that you might regain your sight and be filled with the Holy Spirit."*

Something like fish scales fell from Saul's eyes, and he could see once more. He arose and was baptized. He ate food, and his strength returned.

After spending a few days with the disciples of Damascus, Saul went to the synagogue and started preaching that Jesus was the Son of God. Everyone was amazed because they knew that Saul was one who was AGAINST Jesus. Saul became even more strengthened in his preaching, and those who listened to him were confounded, which proved that Jesus was the Christ (verse 22).

The Jews did not like this, though. They talked among themselves and plotted to kill Saul. The plot was revealed to Saul. Some disciples lowered him down the wall in a basket at night so he could get away.

BIBLE APPLICATION

{Ask:}

- What type of person was Saul BEFORE he met Jesus? [He persecuted the church; he was a Jewish leader.]
- What type of person was Saul AFTER he met Jesus? [He became a missionary for the church and spread the name of Jesus as the Messiah.]
- What types of behaviors, or characteristics, do people show before meeting Jesus? [Read Ephesians 4:17-19.]
- How should people behave once they are in Christ? [Read Ephesians 4:20-32.]

How we used to do things, or used to live, should change. The things we watch on TV, the books we read, the words we say, the actions we do, and the activities we are involved in should change to reflect Jesus to those around us. Remember, the Holy Spirit dwells inside those who decide to follow Jesus with their whole hearts. The Holy Spirit is the One who helps us to live the changed life found in Ephesians.

{Show the vase.}

Jesus called Saul a vessel that He had chosen and was going to use. Saul wrote a letter to the Corinthians where he talked about being a vessel. I wonder if he was thinking about the words Jesus used when Saul was dramatically saved. He wrote about how God causes the light to come from the darkness, and how the light shines from our hearts because we know God. Then he calls us earthen vessels which hold this treasure, this knowledge, this power from God.

{Many people think that Jesus changed Saul's name to Paul when he was on the road to Damascus. This is not true. Jesus spoke in Hebrew and called him *Saul*. The name *Paul* is not used until Acts 13, and it is Luke (the writer of Acts) who does the name change. *Saul* is the man's name in Hebrew, while *Paul* is the same name in Greek. Luke probably started using Paul's Greek name when their ministry to the Gentiles began.}

Later, Saul (AKA Paul) told Timothy how to become a vessel of honor by fleeing thoughts and actions of immaturity and pursuing righteousness. That is what God wants from us. Righteousness, faith, love, and peace will allow us to be vessels, or instruments, ready to do good works for Jesus, just like Saul eventually did.

{Ask:}

- Have YOU had an encounter with Jesus? [Allow for answers, or lead children to close their eyes and listen to you. If the Spirit is leading, present the gospel. See the Extra Resources section for guidance if needed.]

You should know if you have encountered Jesus. There should be no question. If there is a question, then talk to God to see if you really have met Jesus. You must believe that Jesus is the Son of God as well.

Saul asked Jesus what he was to do, which tells us that Saul was ready to surrender everything he was and had to Jesus. Saul fasted for three days waiting to hear from God. He knew he had been wrong. Saul was humble, and he waited to hear what God required of him. After we meet Jesus, we should be ready to confess whatever wrongs we have done and surrender everything we are to Jesus. Then we can eagerly await to see how we can serve Him.

Once Ananias came and told Saul what Jesus expected of him, Saul regained his sight and was filled with the Holy Spirit. Saul publicly showed his new life in Christ through baptism and telling others that Jesus is the Son of God.

What can we learn from the conversion of Saul? If you have a new life in Christ, then you are filled with the Holy Spirit as well. Be public about your change of life. Jesus wants to use you as a vessel. He wants to pour Himself into you so that you can pour yourself into others by loving, serving, and sharing Jesus with them.

COMMENT BOX

■ ■

THINK: What went well as you taught this lesson? What can you do better?

_____

_____

_____

_____

_____

_____

_____

_____

_____

_____

TIP: This is a good lesson to use to present the gospel. See the Extra Resources for tips and follow-up. You might want to consider giving a copy of *Mateo's Choice* to those who make a decision to follow Jesus.

9 PETER AND CORNELIUS

■ ■

The spread of Christianity threatened the status quo of the day. The events that take place in Acts 10 teach us that not only did Christianity go against the idols and gods of the empire, but it also threatened the traditions of Jews. Use this Bible lesson about Peter and Cornelius to teach children how God shows no partiality or favoritism.

Scripture Focus: Acts 10

{Read the Scripture in sections or use storytelling as you go through the interactive questions.}

Materials:

- Pictures of people who need to hear the gospel (I used information from The Seed Company, a nonprofit company that seeks to translate the Bible into heart languages. Examples are the Cicipu language, Amuzgos language, and Micronesian languages. You can watch videos as well. See Resources Page.)
- Small blanket
- Various stuffed animals (Try to use animals that would have been in the sheet, such as a snake, a pig, etc.)
- Acts 10:34-35 poster

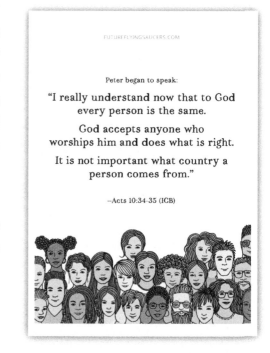

FUTUREFLYINGSAUCERS.COM

Peter began to speak:

"I really understand now that to God every person is the same.

God accepts anyone who worships him and does what is right.

It is not important what country a person comes from."

—Acts 10:34-35 (ICB)

{To prepare, put the animals in the blanket and then bring the four corners together to hide what is inside.}

Geography: Israel; Joppa; Caesarea

Background: Persecution of the early church had begun with the death of Stephen. Christians had fled from Jerusalem. Saul, the great persecutor, had been converted and accepted by the leaders of the new church movement, but Gentiles were still not seen as people who needed Jesus.

OBJECT AND BIBLE LESSON

■ ■ ■ ■ ■ ■ ■ ■ ■ ■ ■ ■ ■ ■ ■ ■ ■ ■ ■

{Show the videos or hold up the pictures of people who are without the Word of God. Ask:}

- How can these people learn about Jesus if they have no Bible? [Allow for answers. Describe how missionaries learn different languages by taking lessons or learning from the people themselves; then they can write the Bible in the heart language (the language spoken most of the time) of the people. You can also mention that some people (especially in the Middle East) have visions and dreams of Jesus coming to them.]

{This is a neat event because we get to see what God is doing in two different places at the same time. Chapter 10 is a long chapter that is PACKED with many details. This lesson does not need fancy story-telling tips because the verses are rich enough in themselves. I suggest reading the chapter from the Bible using the NASB, ESV, or ICB version and answering the following questions. Be sure to read with enthusiasm and wonder! Hand motions (such as gesturing to the sky and pulling your hand down to designate the sheet of animals) are good as well. Read Acts 10 and then ask:}

- What do we learn about Cornelius? [He lived in Caesarea, a centurion of the Italian Regiment, a devout man, he and his household feared God, he was generous, prayed to God always]

- What happened in Cornelius' dream (or vision)? [An angel came and said Cornelius' prayers and alms had come up for a memorial before God. He was to send men to Joppa to find Simon Peter, who was lodging with Simon the Tanner by the sea. Peter would tell Cornelius what to do.]

- How did Cornelius respond to his dream? [He called two servants and a devout soldier, explained everything to them, and sent them to Joppa. This would have been a two-day trip.]

****MEANWHILE...in Joppa...

{Bring out the full blanket. Ask the following questions as you unwrap it and describe what Peter would have seen.}

- Where was Peter and what happened? [He was staying with Simon the Tanner. He was on the roof waiting for lunch when he fell into a trance.]

- What did Peter see? [A sheet came down from heaven, and it was filled with four-footed animals, wild beasts, creeping things, and birds. A voice told Peter to rise, kill, and eat; Peter refused, saying he had never eaten anything that Scripture called unclean.]

- What did the voice say after Peter respectfully said, *"No!"*? [*What God has cleansed, you must not call common.*]

- How many times did this vision take place? [Three times, which means great emphasis from God, or perhaps it reflects Peter's denial of Jesus before the cross]

****MEANWHILE...downstairs...

- Who stood before the gate? [The men sent by Cornelius]

- What was Peter doing when the Spirit spoke to him? [Thinking about the vision]

- What did the Spirit say to Peter? [*Three men are looking for you. Go down to them and go with them. Doubt nothing; I have sent them.*]

****The MEETING...

- Did Peter obey God? [Yes!]

- How? [He asked the men what they needed, housed them for the night, and then left with them in the morning.]

- What had Cornelius done while waiting? [He had called together his relatives and close friends.]

- What did Cornelius do when he met Peter? [He fell at Peter's feet and started to worship him.]

- How did Peter react to Cornelius? [He lifted Cornelius up and told him he was just a man. They talked with each other and entered the house.]

- What did Peter say was unlawful? [It was unlawful for a Jewish man to visit with, or go to, a man of another nationality.]

- But what did God say? [God said that Peter should not call any man common or unclean.]

- What truth did Peter learn? [God shows no partiality. Whoever fears God and works righteousness is accepted by Him.]

- How did Peter preach the gospel? [He told the people that Jesus was Lord of all, that Jesus had been anointed by the Holy Spirit, that Jesus did good things and healings, that Jesus died on a tree, that God raised him from the dead after three days, that Jesus was seen publicly but not by all people, and that whoever believes in Jesus will receive forgiveness of sins.]

- What happened while Peter was speaking? [The Holy Spirit fell upon everyone who heard.]

- Why were the people who came with Peter astonished? [They were astonished because the Holy Spirit had been given to Gentiles. There were six people who had traveled with Peter from Joppa along with Cornelius' men.]

- How did they know the Gentiles had been given the Holy Spirit? [The people had begun to speak in tongues and magnify God.]

- What did Peter then have the Gentiles do? [Be baptized in the name of the Lord]

LIFE APPLICATION

{Show the pictures of people from other nations.}

Peter learned that all people, Jews and Gentiles, need to hear about Jesus Christ. God shows no partiality, but people do. The words of Peter revolutionized culture in that day. For generations Jews had had nothing to do with Gentiles. God was teaching His people that He considers ALL people acceptable to Him through Jesus.

The missionary Paul helps us to understand this better with the words he wrote to the Galatians: *"There is neither Jew nor Greek, there is neither slave nor free man, there is neither male nor female; for you are all one in Christ Jesus."* (Galatians 3:28)

Christianity is an equalizer. Many people live with an attitude that Christians are better than others, or that it is not worth taking the time to tell some other group of people about Jesus. These are lies.

Many unbelievers think that all Christians are "out to get" those who do not believe as they do. Christians must be SURE that they have the heart of God. God loves ALL people. ALL people need to hear about Jesus, and ALL Christians are told to spread the gospel.

{Ask:}

- Can you think of someone who is different than you who needs to know about Jesus? [Allow for answers; you might want to write down the names and begin a prayer list for their salvation. Help the children to brainstorm ideas for how they can share the gospel with their person.]

What can we learn from Peter and Cornelius? All people are equal and acceptable in God's eyes through Jesus. God shows no partiality. All people start out as sinners, and they are dead in their sins. To God, people are unclean, or unrighteous. When you choose to follow Jesus and ask Him to cleanse you of your sins, then you are clean, or righteous, before God.

COMMENT BOX

██ █ █ █ █ █ █ █ █ █ █ █ █ █ █ █ █ █ █ █

THINK: What went well as you taught this lesson? What can you do better?

_____

_____

_____

_____

_____

_____

_____

_____

_____

_____

TIP: This is a good lesson to use in order to teach children to appreciate, understand, and love people who are different than themselves. Be sure to reiterate that all people sin and all people are loved by God, which means Christians are to show love to all people as well.

10 PETER, KING HEROD, AND ANGELS

■ ■

How much do you know about angels? Use this Bible lesson about Peter, King Herod, and angels to discuss the purpose of angels and the meaning of selfless, fervent prayer.

Scripture Focus: Acts 12

Materials:

- Different angels or pictures of angels you might have around the house (Consider any Christmas decorations you might have.)
- Acts 12:11 poster

Geography: Israel; Antioch; Jerusalem; Caesarea; Tyre; Sidon

Background: Saul, the great persecutor, had been converted and accepted by the leaders of the new church movement. Gentiles were still not seen as people who needed Jesus. After a vision, Peter had been brought to Caesarea by Cornelius, the centurion, where Peter learned the truth that Gentiles can be filled with the same Holy Spirit as Jews. When Peter returned to Jerusalem, he informed the church leaders of what had happened, and they welcomed the new converts to the early church.

FUTUREFLYINGSAUCERS.COM

Then Peter realized what had happened. He thought,

"Now I know that the Lord really sent his angel to me. He rescued me from Herod and from all the things the Jewish people thought would happen."

–Acts 12:11 (ICB)

Men who had been dispersed because of the persecution found themselves in Antioch preaching the gospel. Many people turned to the Lord, and Barnabas was sent up to investigate and teach. He went to Tarsus and got Saul, and they both stayed in Antioch to teach the people. People began to be called *Christians* in Antioch. After a year, Saul and Barnabas traveled to Jerusalem to take money to the believers there because there was a famine.

If you aren't sure what you think about angels, see the Resources Page for some information to consider.

OBJECT AND BIBLE LESSON

{Show the angels and talk about how they are the same or different. Are they lifelike? Or cartoonish?}

- What facts do you know about angels? [Have the children list everything they know. Discuss fact versus opinion, tradition, or artists' rendering. Be sure to talk about people to whom angels have appeared, what they said, and what they did. You will probably find that many perceptions are skewed and worldly. Keep in mind that in the Scriptures, angels are described with and without wings.]

In Acts 12, an angel appears two times and does two very different actions.

{Read or tell the story from Acts 12:1-19.}

King Herod, in Jerusalem, decided to "mistreat" those in the early church. He seized James, the brother of John, and had him killed by the sword. When he saw that the Jews were pleased by his actions, he seized Peter and put him in jail to await the same fate. However, Passover was about to take place, so the death of Peter would have to wait. Peter sat in jail with 16 guards around him.

{Ask:}

- How did the church pray for Peter? [Constant prayer; fervently]
- Why do you think they were praying like that? [Allow for answers. Maybe they were scared. Herod was harassing and killing people in the church; they did not want that for Peter.]

The night before Peter was to go before Herod, Peter was asleep in his jail cell, bound to two soldiers. Guards were outside his door. Suddenly an angel appeared in the jail cell. He struck Peter by knocking him on his side. The chains fell off of Peter, and the angel told him to get his shoes, put on his cloak, and follow him. Peter obeyed, thinking he was having a vision.

They passed by the first set of guards, and then another set. They reached the city, and the gate opened by itself. They walked down the street, and the angel left.

{Ask:}

> • What did Peter think had happened? [He thought it was all a dream until he found himself alone by the open gate.]

Peter went to the house where all of the people were praying. The house belonged to Mary, the mother of John Mark (who wrote the gospel of Mark). Peter knocked on the door. A servant girl named Rhoda answered it. She recognized Peter's voice, and because of her excitement, she left the gate closed and ran back to the praying Christians. She announced who was at the gate, but no one believed her. They said it was probably Peter's angel.

{It is interesting that this term was used, but it is not the same reference used for the angel who let Peter out of jail. This term is referring to a resurrected body and was used when Jesus appeared after rising from the dead. A person does not turn into an angel when he dies, but he is given a resurrected body through Jesus Christ.}

Peter continued to knock until they let him in. They were amazed! He asked them to be quiet—after all, he had just escaped from jail! He told them about the angel and his escape, and asked them to tell James and the others. Peter then left to go to another place.

{If you recall, James, the brother of John, is dead. There was also James, the half-brother of Jesus. He was one of the three pillars of the Jewish church. He wrote the book of James.}

{Ask:}

> • What was the result of Peter being led out of jail? [Morning came, and quite the commotion took place! Herod searched for Peter and could not find him. He interrogated the guards and ordered their execution. Herod, in his anger, left town and went to his palace by the sea in Caesarea.]

{Read or tell Acts 12: 20-24.}

Herod was angry about Peter disappearing. He was also angry with the people of the cities of Tyre and Sidon. The people did not want Herod to be angry with them. On an appointed day, Herod dressed up in fine clothes and gave speeches to the people. While he spoke, the people called out, *"The voice of a god and not of man!"*

Immediately an angel struck him.

{Ask:}

- Wow! Why do you think an angel struck Herod? [Herod was not giving glory to God, but to himself, when he allowed the people to exclaim those words.]
- What was the result of the angel striking Herod? [Herod was eaten by worms and died.]

Then Saul, Barnabas, and John Mark returned to Antioch.

LIFE APPLICATION

██ █ █ █ █ █ █ █ █ █ █ █ █ █ █ █ █ █ █

{Show the angels again.}

- Have you learned anything new about angels from this chapter in Acts? [Allow for answers. Angels have power. Angels can cause death. Angels bring glory to God.]

- What did the angel(s) do to Peter and to Herod? [Maybe it was the same angel? Or maybe not. Nothing in Scripture alludes to both sightings being the same angel; it only refers to the same type of being. But in both cases, an angel struck a man. One person was bringing glory to God; the other was bringing glory to himself.]

Angels stand for God. They are the Lord's. They are real.

We should ponder the amount of prayer that took place during this amazing jailbreak. The Christians were praying with fervor. *Fervor* means an intense and passionate feeling. Those people were on their faces before God. God heard them!

God moves when people pray. "Now I lay me down to sleep" prayers are OK, but fervent prayers before God seem to change the world.

{Ask:}

- What do you think makes a fervent prayer? [Allow for answers. Encourage the use of words such as confession, praising God, asking for forgiveness, specific prayers, trusting God with the answers, and selfless prayers.]

What can we learn from Peter, Herod, and the angels? We can either glorify ourselves, something else, or God. The whole purpose of man is to glorify God and make Him known to others. If we substitute something else for God, then He might find a way to show us that we do not have our priorities in order. Fervent prayer and putting God first will change the world, especially when we focus on sharing the gospel with others.

COMMENT BOX

THINK: What went well as you taught this lesson? What can you do better?

_____

_____

_____

_____

_____

_____

_____

_____

_____

TIP: Practice prayer with your children. The more children pray and listen to prayers of adults, the more they learn how to communicate with God on their own.

11 PAUL BEGINS THE FIRST MISSIONARY JOURNEY

■ ■

People will either choose God or something else. Use this Bible lesson from Acts 13 about Paul's first missionary journey to discuss the Wordless Book and how people will try to stop us from telling others about the gospel.

Scripture Focus: Acts 13:1-39

Materials:

- Create a Wordless Book if you do not have one already (or use a bracelet or other form of telling the gospel with the colors). I recommend not using the color black in reference to sin or evil because of racial considerations. Consider using a brown or dark grey color and saying stained or unrighteous instead of black. Use the colors red, white (or light grey), blue, green, and gold. See the Resources Page for a video example.)

- Acts 13:2 poster

Geography: Israel; Antioch; Jerusalem; Seleucia; Cyprus; Paphos; Perga; Antioch in Pisidia

Background: Saul, the great persecutor, had been converted and accepted by the leaders of the new church movement. Peter had had a vision and learned that Greeks and Gentiles were to be a part of the new church. The believers spread from Jerusalem to Samaria, Ethiopia, and Antioch, and there were many who did not like this new religion.

OBJECT AND BIBLE LESSON

{Read or tell the events of Acts 13:1-12.}

After Peter was released from jail, Saul (Paul) and Barnabas returned to Antioch with John Mark, who was a cousin of Barnabas. The church leaders in Antioch prayed and fasted as they ministered to the Lord. The Holy Spirit told them to separate out Saul and Barnabas for work. The men continued to fast and pray. They laid hands on Saul and Barnabas and sent them out as God called them.

{Hold up the Wordless Book, whichever form you are using. Ask the children if they recognize it and if they know what the colors mean. Explain that these books are used to preach the gospel, just like Saul preached the gospel.}

These men, along with John Mark, began the first missionary journey. They went to Cyprus and stopped at the synagogues to preach the word of God. When they went to the town of Paphos, they met a sorcerer named Bar-Jesus. This man was with the leading government official, Sergius Paulus, an intelligent man.

Sergius Paulus called for Saul because he wanted to hear the word of God. But the sorcerer somehow withstood Saul and Barnabas because he wanted to turn the proconsul away from the faith.

{Ask:}

- Why do you think Bar-Jesus wanted to influence the proconsul? [Allow for answers. The Bible does not tell us the reason, but think of the times when Jesus or Paul were casting out demons. The demons knew who Jesus was, and they knew not to mess with Him. God's enemy knows that when people turn to God, their lives will change, and Satan will have no power over them anymore.]

{When you quote Paul, be dramatic!}

At this point, the Bible begins to call Saul, *Paul*. Paul, who was filled with the Holy Spirit, turned to Bar-Jesus, looked intensely at him, and said, *"You son of the devil! You are an enemy of everything that is right! You are full of evil tricks and lies. You are always trying to change the Lord's truths into lies! Now the Lord will touch you, and you will be blind. For a time you will not be able to see anything—not even the light from the sun."* (Acts 13:10-11, ICB)

Immediately the sorcerer could not see. The government official believed and was astonished at the teaching of the Lord.

{Read or tell the events of Acts 13:13-15.}

Paul, Barnabas, and John Mark went on to Perga. Then John Mark returned to Jerusalem, and the other two went on to Antioch in Pisidia (not the same Antioch they had left from).

{Ask:}

- Where did Paul and Barnabas go first to share the gospel? [The synagogue]
- Who goes to the synagogue? [The Jews]

The two men went to the synagogue, and after the readings were done, one of the rulers of the synagogue asked them if they had any words for the people. Paul stood up and started to preach. He began with the Old Testament Scriptures about Israel being brought out of captivity in Egypt. He spoke of taking the land for their nation, and of Samuel, King Saul, and King David. Then he started talking about Jesus.

{Hold up the Wordless Book and point to the colors as Paul told the gospel.}

"Darkness" color - We need to repent from sin (verses 23-24).

Red - Salvation has been given. Jesus died on the cross and was raised three days later. Red represents the blood of Jesus (verses 28-32).

Light color - We have forgiveness of sins and have been cleansed (verses 38-39).

{Explain that baptism (blue), Christian growth (green), and going to heaven (gold) happen after belief in Jesus. Many times, people need to hear the message of the gospel a few times before their hearts are opened to Jesus.}

After Paul had preached, the Gentiles begged to have him preach again the next week. Many began to follow Paul. The next week he preached again in the synagogue. Almost the entire city came to hear Paul preach.

However, when the Jews saw the crowd, they became jealous and started speaking against Paul and his teachings. Paul and Barnabas became bold and stated, *"You were to receive the message of God first. But since you reject it, and consider yourselves unworthy of eternal life, then we turn to the Gentiles!"*

When the Gentiles heard this, they were overjoyed! They glorified the Lord, and many were saved. The word of the Lord continued to spread.

As for the Jews, they continued to stir up controversy and attempted to persecute Paul and Barnabas. The men shook the dust off their shoes as they left town and traveled to Iconium.

LIFE APPLICATION

Two times when Paul and Barnabas were preaching the gospel, people tried to stop them. The first time, Paul knew the man was a sorcerer and called him out; he said the man was full of deceit, a son of the devil, and an enemy of righteousness. These words may seem pretty strong to us, but Paul knew who he was dealing with.

What exactly *IS* a sorcerer? Some people would say a witch, someone of dark magic, or someone who says spells. Are people like this really real?

There are some people who pretend to be sorcerers so they can get money, such as palm readers or fortune tellers. Then there are others, like this sorcerer whom Paul dealt with, who are part of something beyond themselves that is not of God.

When it comes to the gospel, people are either on God's side or they are not. People have a hard time with this truth. Think back to the garden of Eden. Who influenced Eve to eat of the fruit and disobey God? (Satan) Satan is against God, and he always will be. He wants to turn people away from faith in Jesus.

The second time, Paul was stopped by the Jews from preaching the gospel. The Jews were (and still are) God's chosen people. They love God, but they do not accept Jesus as their Messiah.

{Take this opportunity to use the Wordless Book again to explain and present the gospel. You might want to have the children tell you what the colors represent to see if they can explain the gospel themselves.}

What can we learn from Paul beginning his first missionary journey? God loves us. That is what the gospel message tells us. God is also holy, and we must deal with sin. The gospel tells us that as well. It is always good to be ready to share the gospel. Jesus died for a reason. God's grace covers us through the blood of Jesus. If we do not have that blood on us, then we do not have a right relationship with God the Father. We either believe in Jesus or we do not. There is no middle ground.

COMMENT BOX

■ ■ ■ ■ ■ ■ ■ ■ ■ ■ ■ ■ ■ ■ ■ ■ ■ ■

THINK: What went well as you taught this lesson? What can you do better?

_____

_____

_____

_____

_____

_____

_____

_____

_____

TIP: Never grow weary of sharing the gospel with your children. You never know when the Holy Spirit will be working in a little one's heart.

12 PERSEVERANCE OF PAUL

■ ■

How should we handle life when hard situations come our way? Use this fun object lesson from Acts 14 to teach how Paul and Barnabas endured and persisted to share the gospel.

Scripture Focus: Acts 14

Materials:

- Paper towel tube (or 2 toilet paper tubes taped together)
- 1 piece of copy paper
- Tape

- 2-3 heavy books (not encyclopedias, but do not use thin children's books)
- Acts 14:22 poster

Geography: Israel; Antioch; Jerusalem; Iconium; Lystra; Derbe; Pisidia; Pamphylia; Perga; Attalia

Background: After Peter was released from jail, Saul and Barnabas returned to Antioch with John Mark, who was a cousin of Barnabas. They were sent off on the first missionary journey. The Jews would hear the gospel first and then the Gentiles. Eventually Paul stated that the Jews had rejected the gospel and that he would preach to the Gentiles. The word of the Lord continued to spread. As for the Jews, they continued to stir up controversy and attempted to persecute Paul and Barnabas.

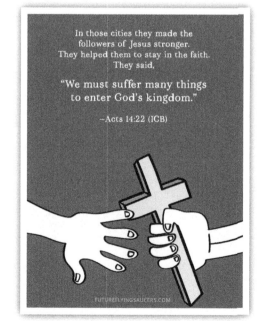

In those cities they made the followers of Jesus stronger. They helped them to stay in the faith. They said,

"We must suffer many things to enter God's kingdom."

—Acts 14:22 (ICB)

FUTUREFLYINGSAUCERS.COM

OBJECT LESSON

{Have all the materials in front of you.}

This tube is going to represent Jesus.

{Stand the tube on end.}

Jesus is all-powerful. When He was on earth, He had to persevere under trials. Men were mean to Him. He was accused of blasphemy (saying He was equal with God). Jesus was whipped, beaten, and mocked. He had a crown of thorns stuck into His head. Finally, He was put on a cross and left to die. He died. At any point Jesus could have flown off, disappeared, called down fire from heaven, or asked for angels to attack...but He did not. Jesus chose to endure the pressure of being treated unfairly and wrong.

{Carefully place the books, one at a time, onto the top end of the tube. The tube should withstand the weight of the books.}

Jesus had the strength to persevere under horrible circumstances. These books are heavy, just like the pressure and bad circumstances Jesus underwent. But He was able to endure to the end. After three days in the tomb, Jesus rose from the grave. He conquered death, allowing any who believe in Him to have eternal life.

BIBLE LESSON

That is the message of the gospel that Paul and Barnabas took to as many towns and cities that they could.

{Read or tell Acts 14:1-7. Ask:}

- Where did Paul and Barnabas go first when they entered the town? [The synagogue]

- Whom did they speak to? [They spoke to the Jews at first, but they must have spoken so well that a multitude formed; both Jews and Greeks believed.]

- What happened when Paul stayed longer? [They spoke boldly, bearing witness to God's word and granting signs and wonders.]

- Why did people want to stone them? [Because the town was divided]

Paul and Barnabas went to **Iconium.** They went to the synagogue first, and many Jews and Greeks believed. But there were a handful of Jews who stirred up trouble and poisoned the minds of the people against Paul. The two men stayed for quite some time, teaching and working signs and wonders. Many people believed, but the town was divided: Jews versus the apostles. Word came to Paul and Barnabas that a violent attempt (stoning) on their lives was going to take place, and they fled to Lystra.

{Read Acts 14:8-28.}

- Who do we meet in this Scripture section? [A crippled man and the priest of Zeus]

- What do we know about the crippled man? [He had no strength in his feet. He was sitting. He had not been able to walk since birth. He had been listening to Paul speak. The man had been watched by Paul.]

- What did Paul observe about the crippled man? [He saw that the man had faith to be healed.]

- How do you think Paul knew that? [Allow for answers. When people are led by the Holy Spirit, He gives spiritual discernment when needed.]

In **Lystra**, Paul and Barnabas continued to preach the gospel. There was a man who had been crippled since birth. He had been listening to Paul. Paul recognized that this man had the faith to be healed. In a loud voice Paul said, *"Stand up to your feet!"* The man jumped up and was healed. When the people in town saw this, they thought their gods, Zeus and Hermes, had come down to earth.

The priest for Zeus started to bring oxen and garlands because he was going to sacrifice to Paul and Barnabas. When the two men heard this, they tore their garments and ran through the crowds. They exclaimed that they were just mere men, but that they preached for the Living God who created the world and made the rain. Paul and Barnabas barely restrained the people from sacrificing to them.

{Ask:}

- Why did Paul and Barnabas stress to the people that it was the Living God who had created everything, including the rain? [A statue, or a story, is not what created the world or blesses the fields with rain. It is the Living God who cares for people and provides what we need to live. He is the One who should be worshiped.]

Then a handful of Jews came from Iconium and started to persuade the crowds against Paul. They even stoned him, dragged him outside the city, and left him for dead. When the disciples came to Paul and surrounded him, Paul stood up and went back into the city.

{Ask:}

- Why do you think Paul went back to the city? [Allow for answers.]

{Take the books off the tube if you have not already.}

- What will happen if I try to put the books on top of this sheet of paper? [Allow for answers.]

{Hold the paper on its edge and try to put the books on it. Show that there is no way for a sheet of paper on its edge to hold the books.}

- Of whom was Paul full? [Jesus and the Holy Spirit]

{Remind the children that the tube represents Jesus. Take the sheet of

paper and wrap it around the tube. Use a piece of tape to hold the paper. Put the tube and paper on end and place the books on top.}

When we are filled with Jesus and the Holy Spirit, then we can endure whatever life throws at us. It will not be easy, but we can do it with Jesus' power.

{Ask:}

- Why did Paul get up and go back into the town after being stoned? [He was full of the Holy Spirit. He knew that he needed to preach the gospel to whomever would listen.]

The next day, Paul and Barnabas left for **Derbe**. They preached in this town and made many disciples. Then Paul and Barnabas went back to Lystra, Iconium, and Antioch to strengthen the churches there. Paul told the people that they would endure many tribulations. Paul and Barnabas fasted, prayed, and appointed elders in the churches; then they traveled on to Pisidia, Paphylia, Perga, Attalia, and then back to Antioch where they originally had started.

The two men reported everything that had happened on their journey and how faith had come to the Gentiles. Paul and Barnabas stayed there for some time.

LIFE APPLICATION

■ ■

Paul believed in the gospel. He believed THE gospel. He knew that it was the truth. Paul knew that God had called him to proclaim the gospel to the ends of the earth. Paul was **persistent and persevered**. He did not give up. In this chapter of Acts, violent Jews and a stoning did not persuade him to stop telling the gospel. He literally got back up and went into the town again. Usually it was other disciples who urged him to leave and go to the next city. However, Paul returned to the cities that had wanted him dead to minister to the disciples and set up the new churches.

{Ask:}

- How determined are you to tell the gospel to others? [Allow for answers. Guide the children to think of people they have shared the gospel with in the past. If they have never shared the gospel before, turn to the previous lesson and have the children practice with the Wordless Book.]

What can we learn from the persistence of Paul? How persistent are you? Maybe you shared the gospel once and it wasn't received well. Paul was humiliated at times, but he continued on because he knew that eternal souls were at stake. Paul also understood that some people would accept the gospel, and others would reject it. However, he knew it was his job to tell the gospel to everyone no matter what happened. You might have family or friends who need to hear the gospel. Perhaps you have already spoken to them once. Be persistent. Do not give up. Continue to pray for their salvation and ask God to give you the words to say. He will never let you down!

COMMENT BOX

████████████████████████

THINK: What went well as you taught this lesson? What can you do better?

_____

_____

_____

_____

_____

_____

_____

_____

TIP: Children must practice sharing the gospel. Group the children in pairs and have them practice telling the gospel using the Wordless Book. Then ask for volunteers who are willing to present the gospel to the group. Consider having the children make a bracelet with beads the colors of the Wordless Book so they have something with them to help them explain the gospel to family and friends.

13 THE COUNCIL OF JERUSALEM

■ ■ ■ ■ ■ ■ ■ ■ ■ ■ ■ ■ ■ ■ ■ ■ ■ ■ ■ ■

What does a life changed because of Jesus actually look like? Use this object lesson about the Council of Jerusalem to discuss salvation, grace, and life change.

Scripture Focus: Acts 15

Materials:

- A pile of blocks labeled with different laws (I had 13 blocks and used the website listed on the Resources Page to find the laws. Be sure the blocks are big enough to become heavy after holding them a while.)
- A white or red scarf
- Acts 15:8 poster

Geography: Israel; Antioch; Jerusalem

Background: The word of the Lord continued to spread. As for the Jews, they continued to stir up controversy and attempted to persecute Paul and Barnabas. Paul and Barnabas completed their first missionary journey and stayed in Antioch.

{This chapter of Acts involves the topic of circumcision. Depending upon the age of the children you teach, you might want to be vague about the meaning of the law. You do not want to lose the group because

FUTUREFLYINGSAUCERS.COM

God, who knows the thoughts of all men, accepted them. He showed this to us by giving them the Holy Spirit, just as he did to us.

−Acts 15:8 (ICB)

they are giggling or embarrassed about the topic. In this lesson I chose to be vague. If you have children who are mature enough to handle it, you can use more specific terms. Please do not use diagrams or visual aid examples!}

OBJECT LESSON

{Have a student volunteer come to the front of the group.}

Remember that the Jews were given laws from God. Among those laws were the Ten Commandments. God gave them these laws so they would become His nation and be different from the surrounding nations. There were also many other laws that the Jews were to keep. There was nothing wrong with these laws. They were from God and were good things to do.

{Begin reading out the laws you put on the blocks as you stack them in the arms of the student.}

The Jews were to obey these rules every day, or whenever God had told them to do a particular law, such as the festivals. These were commands, not options. Keep in mind, though, that over the years, Jewish leadership had added more laws to the original laws God gave to Israel.

{Tell the student to stand and hold the laws while you tell the story. You will find that the "laws" become heavy.}

BIBLE LESSON

Paul and Barnabas were in Antioch after their first missionary journey. While they were there, a man began to preach in the area of Judea. He told the people that they must follow certain laws of the Jews in order to be saved. This really bothered Paul and Barnabas. They attempted to argue with this man. All of those involved decided that they should go up to Jerusalem and take the matter before the apostles and elders.

When Paul and Barnabas arrived in Jerusalem, they told the council about their travels and what they had experienced. Everyone was overjoyed until a few followers of Jesus, who were also Pharisees, rose up and exclaimed that the Gentiles must follow the law of Moses.

{Check on the student to see if the laws (blocks) are heavy. Have him continue standing and holding the blocks. This is a great way to get some humor into the lesson!}

Peter stood up before the group and explained that the Gentiles had received grace just as the Jews had. (Remember Peter's vision and experience with Cornelius?) He explained that God knows a person's heart. Then he asked why the leaders would want to put the same yoke upon the Gentiles as the Jews had, even when the Jews themselves could not bear the laws.

Then Paul and Barnabas spoke about their experiences with God and the Gentiles.

Then James, the brother of Jesus and most probably the author of the New Testament book *James*, answered that the Gentiles should not be bothered with the Jewish laws. He went on to explain that a letter should be written explaining what they *should* do, though. Gentiles were to stay away from anything having to do with idols, things that were strangled, and blood; they were to remain pure.

A letter was written. Paul and Barnabas, along with a few friends, Judas and Silas, took the letter to Antioch to read it to the brethren. All rejoiced. They stayed there for some time; then Judas went back to Jerusalem, but Silas stayed. The men taught and encouraged the people of the church.

{Check on the student again. Have him continue holding the blocks.}

LIFE APPLICATION

{Ask:}

- Are those blocks of the Law heavy? [Yes]
- Do you think you could hold them every day as you go about your daily business? [No]

The Law is heavy. The yoke that oxen wear around their necks when plowing is heavy. Jesus said for us to give Him our yoke and take His instead.

{Take the blocks from the student. Put the scarf in his hands or over his shoulders. Ask:}

- The scarf is God's grace. Is it lighter? [Yes]
- Jesus said that He came to fulfill the Law. Is there any way we can keep the Law perfectly every day? [No]

That is why we need grace. God knows we cannot follow the Law perfectly. We make mistakes. Sometimes we choose to disobey the Law. The Law was given by God to the Jews so they could be a people set apart, holy, for Him. The Law was to make the Jews righteous. The Jews failed miserably. Just read the Old Testament!

Jesus *can* keep the Law, though. All we have to do is believe in Jesus and confess our sins, and then we are considered righteous (I John 1:9). Jesus fulfills all the requirements of the Law. Once we believe in Jesus and choose to follow Him, since He fulfills all of the requirements, does that mean we can go and break all of the Ten Commandments? Oh, no.

{Point to the scarf.}

Remember grace? When we are covered by grace, it helps us to want to obey God.

When we remember that Jesus died on the cross for us, we should want to obey God and His commandments. Do we obey all of them? All 613 of the laws? No.

Remember what the Jerusalem Council said? We are to stay away from idols, stay away from strangled things, stay away from drinking or eating blood, and remain pure.

The first three requirements had to do with idol worship. The fourth tells us that we need to keep our minds and bodies pure; that comes with obeying the moral laws of God which Jesus taught. (These include the heart of the Ten Commandments, such as anger and lust.)

The greatest commandment is to love your God with all your heart, with all your soul, and with all your might. The second commandment is like it: Love your neighbor as yourself. All of the laws are reflected in those two. When you encounter Jesus and choose to follow Him, His grace will motivate you to live the way God wants you to live.

What can we learn from the Jerusalem Council? Salvation is for Jews AND Gentiles. With salvation comes a life change. That means we start living our lives the way God wants instead of how we want. Sometimes that means giving up certain hobbies or behaviors. God cares about your heart and wants it to reflect Him. We are to love God and love people.

COMMENT BOX

■ ■ ■ ■ ■ ■ ■ ■ ■ ■ ■ ■ ■ ■ ■ ■ ■ ■ ■ ■

THINK: What went well as you taught this lesson? What can you do better?

_____

_____

_____

_____

_____

_____

_____

_____

TIP: Remind the children that works do not save us. Only faith in Jesus Christ can save us from our sins. Good works are the evidence of changed lives.

14 PAUL AND SILAS IN PRISON

■ ■

Jesus brings freedom from the chains of sin that bind us. Use this object lesson about Paul and Silas in prison to discuss Acts 16 and see examples of Jesus literally freeing people.

Scripture Focus: Acts 16:16-40

Materials:

- A thick chain (I did not have any, so I bought two feet of chain from my local hardware store for about $8 USD. See the Resources Page for an example.)
- Acts 16:31 Poster

Geography: Philippi

Background: Paul and Barnabas completed their first missionary journey and stayed in Antioch for a while. Paul decided to go back to all of the places he and Barnabas had gone in order to check on the new churches. Paul refused to have John Mark travel with them. Barnabas went on a journey with John Mark, and Paul chose to travel with Silas. Paul went to Lystra and invited Timothy to join them. Then they went to Troas after the Spirit told them not to go to Asia, and a vision sent them to Macedonia. In Philippi they met Lydia, and the church began with her and her household believing in Jesus.

They said to him,

"Believe in the Lord Jesus and you will be saved— you and all the people in your house."

–Acts 16:31 (ICB)

FUTUREFLYINGSAUCERS.COM

OBJECT LESSON

{Show the chain. Ask:}

- What do we use chains for? [Accept answers. Be sure to include describing words such as to hold items down, to keep things from moving, to make things heavy, etc.]

We sing songs, such as a more recent version of "Amazing Grace," with words such as *"My chains are gone, I've been set free!"*

- What do those words mean? [Accept answers.]
- If we sing this song, does that mean we were literally wearing chains? [No]

The Scripture for this lesson is going to help us understand these words better. In fact, these Scriptures show us three ways people can be in chains, or bondage.

{Have a volunteer hold the chain, or pass it around for everyone to hold and feel. Talk about how heavy the chain is. Discuss what it would be like to wear these constantly. Read Acts 16:11-15. Ask:}

- In which town is Paul? [Philippi]
- Who is with him? [Silas, Timothy, and probably Dr. Luke]
- In whose house are they staying? [Lydia's]

<u>Bondage #1:</u>

{Read Acts 16:16-24. Ask:}

Paul and the other men went to prayer.

- Where would that have been? [The river]
- Who followed Paul? [A slave girl]

- What was different about this girl? [This girl was possessed by a demon which allowed her to tell futures. She made a lot of money for her masters.]

Remember, we have talked about how some people "pretend" to be magic, and then there are other people who experience spiritual matters that are real and evil. This girl was in the second group. This was very real. Whether she got involved with demons on her own, or it was an accident, we do not know. The Bible is clear that she had a demon, a spirit of divination, inside her. **She was in bondage to this demon.** She was held down, and she definitely could not be who God wanted her to be.

For days, this slave girl followed Paul around and yelled out, *"These men are servants of the Most High God! They tell about salvation!"*

{Ask:}

- Was the girl telling the truth? [Yes]
- Paul became irritated with her. Why would he get frustrated with her? [Allow answers.]

Paul knew there was an evil spirit in her. Demons know the truth about Jesus, and they try to confuse people about the truth. If someone who had a demon was declaring the truth about Jesus, then people would not need to listen to Paul. This would cause confusion. Therefore, Paul told the spirit to leave the girl.

Bondage #2:

The spirit left the girl immediately. You would think people would be happy about this. The girl was no longer in bondage! No, her masters recognized that the girl would no longer make money for them. They seized Paul and Silas and dragged them into the marketplace. They created a mob of angry people and commanded Paul and Silas to be beaten. Once Paul and Silas had been beaten, they were placed in jail in the stocks. They probably wore chains similar to these.

{Hold up the chain.}

Paul and Silas were in **physical bondage**. They were held down. They did not have freedom.

{Read Acts 16:25-34.}

At midnight Paul and Silas were praying and singing, and the other prisoners were listening to them. There were probably some jailers there as well. Music is a wonderful way to declare the glory of God and encourage people.

{Ask:}

- What happened as they were singing? [An earthquake shook the jail, the doors all opened, and the chains fell off the prisoners]

Bondage #3:

The keeper of the prison ran into the jail. He was ready to fall on his sword because he knew that if prisoners escaped, then he would be killed by his superiors. Paul told him to stop because all of the prisoners were still there. The jailer asked for a light and saw the truth. He fell at the feet of Paul and Silas and asked what he needed to do to be saved. The keeper of the jail, who kept prisoners in chains, **knew that his soul was in chains—in spiritual bondage.**

{Hold up the chain.}

Paul told the man to believe in the Lord Jesus Christ and he would be saved, along with his household. The man did. Paul and Silas preached the gospel to the man's family. The jailer washed Paul and Silas' wounds from the beating. Then the man and his family were baptized.

They were free from the bondage of sin.

The next morning, the leaders of the town sent the message that Paul and Silas were to be set free from the prison. Paul refused to go. He sent a message back to the leaders that he and Silas were Romans who had been beaten without a trial. This was not supposed to happen! It was unlawful for a Roman citizen to be punished without a trial. When they heard that Paul and Silas were Romans, the leaders became afraid and pleaded with them to go quietly and leave the town. Paul and Silas went back to Lydia's house. They encouraged the new church and then left the city.

LIFE APPLICATION

■ ■ ■ ■ ■ ■ ■ ■ ■ ■ ■ ■ ■ ■ ■ ■ ■ ■ ■ ■

There is a line in the "Amazing Grace" song that says, *"My chains are gone! I've been set free!"*

{Play the song if needed. See the Resource Page. Ask:}

- In this song, what chains are we singing about? [The chains of sin]

Once a person believes in the Lord Jesus and is saved, the chains of sin, the yuckiness of sin, the holding down of sin, our sin nature departs from us. Believing in Jesus allows us to stand before God and be free!

- Will we sin again? [Yes]

As we walk with Jesus, we will have sin, such as choices, attitudes, behaviors, and habits that do not reflect Jesus. These sins entangle us like vines around our feet. We might even get entangled and fall because of our sin. With the power of the Holy Spirit, we can untangle ourselves and walk straight again. This is why obeying Jesus, listening to the Holy Spirit, and reading our Bible is so important. Walking in the ways of Jesus and being led by the Holy Spirit help us to stay out of sin. The Bible tells us how to live a righteous and free life. But if we ignore what the Bible says, or make excuses, or make bad choices...then sin can trip us and distract us from following Jesus. We are still saved from our sin nature...but we will not live a life focused on Jesus.

What can we learn from Paul and Silas being in prison? Even though people can be in physical bondage, spiritual bondage is worse. Dealing with sin is important. Knowing how to deal with sin and how to tell others to deal with sin is part of sharing the gospel with others. Jesus brings freedom.

COMMENT BOX

■ ■ ■ ■ ■ ■ ■ ■ ■ ■ ■ ■ ■ ■ ■ ■ ■ ■ ■

THINK: What went well as you taught this lesson? What can you do better?

_____

_____

_____

_____

_____

_____

_____

_____

_____

TIP: Talking about demonic activity with little children can be scary. After all, it can sound like a movie. Keep your lesson age-appropriate and watch the reactions of your children. Demons are just as real today as they were in Bible. This is a subject that should be taught. However, we do need to be sensitive to those whom we teach. Always bring this topic back to Jesus. He is the all-powerful One!

15 PREACHING THE GOSPEL

■ ■ ■ ■ ■ ■ ■ ■ ■ ■ ■ ■ ■ ■ ■ ■ ■ ■ ■ ■

When people hear the gospel, they can respond in different ways. Use this Bible lesson from Acts 17 to discuss how three different cities reacted to Paul's preaching of the gospel.

Scripture Focus: Acts 17

Materials:

- 3-D solids of a cube and a cone (Use the patterns on the Resource Page.)
- Acts 17:11 poster

Geography: Thessalonica; Berea; Athens

Background: Paul is on his second missionary journey with Silas. Paul went to Lystra and invited Timothy to join them. They went to Troas after the Holy Spirit told them to not go to Asia. Then a vision from God sent them to Macedonia. In Philippi, they met Lydia; the church began with her and her household believing in Jesus. After healing a servant girl from a demon, Paul and Silas were put in jail illegally. After the town leaders realized their mistake, they asked Paul and Silas to leave quietly.

These Jews were better than the Jews in Thessalonica. They were eager to hear the things Paul and Silas said.

These Jews in Berea studied the Scriptures every day to find out if these things were true.

–Acts 17:11 (ICB)

OBJECT LESSON

{Hold up the cube. Ask:}

- What is this? [A cube]
- When I hold it this way, what can you see? [Hold it so they can see just a square; then turn it to show it on the point, and then on the edge. Discuss that, for the most part, a cube looks the same or similar from every angle.]

{Hold up the cone. Ask:}

- What is this? [A cone]
- When I hold it different ways, what do you see? [Hold it so only the circle can be seen; then turn it to show the long side, and then the point. Discuss how different each view is.]

If you look at this cone from different perspectives, then it looks different. Even the cube looked slightly different at different points of view, but it was more similar than the cone. The cube was still a cube, and the cone was still a cone even if we looked at them from different angles. Our points of view did not change the truth that we were looking at a cube and a cone.

BIBLE LESSON

{Read Acts 17:1-9.}

Paul, Silas, and Timothy went to Thessalonica. The first place they went was the synagogue. For three Sabbaths, Paul reasoned with the people.

{Ask:}

- What were the results of Paul's preaching at first? [Some were persuaded to believe; a great group of the Greeks believed; many leading women believed; and they all joined Paul and Silas.]
- Who got upset? [The Jews who were not persuaded caused a riot.]
- What were the disciples accused of? [Turning the world upside down]

There was a disciple named Jason. Some jealous Jews attacked his home and dragged Jason and a few others into the city square. Jason was accused of housing the ones who were turning the world upside down. He was also accused of going against the Caesar by saying there was another king named Jesus. Later, Jason and the others were let go after paying money to the city.

{Read Acts 17:10-15.}

Paul and Silas left during the night and went to Berea. Again, they went to the synagogue of the Jews.

- How did this city respond? [The people received the gospel with readiness; they were fair-minded, or noble-minded; they searched the Scriptures for themselves; many Jews believed; many Greeks and prominent women and men believed.]

What a great thing! When the Jews from Thessalonica came to town, they began to stir up the crowd. The new church sent Paul away by ship. Silas and Timothy stayed behind.

{Read Acts 17:16-23; 32-34. Ask:}

- How did Paul feel when he looked around Athens? [Paul looked around the city of Athens and was saddened by the idolatry he saw.]
- Where did Paul go first? [To the synagogue]
- Who wanted to hear more from Paul? [Epicurean and Stoic philosophers]
- What did they call Paul? [A babbler]
- Where did the philosophers take Paul? [The Areopagus]

Paul traveled to Athens. Once he arrived, he sent word back for Silas and Timothy to join him. Paul went to the synagogue and started to reason with the Jews and Gentile worshipers. He also went into the marketplace daily. He had noticed that there was a temple that had been built to The Unknown God. When he was up on the Areopagus, or Mars Hill, he told the people that His God had made all of the stone, gold, or silver used to make their gods. Paul explained that God was the Creator of all things. He told the people to repent and know that the world would be judged by the Man whom God raised from the dead.

{Ask:}

- How did these people respond? [When people heard about the resurrection, some mocked; others asked to hear more; some men joined Paul and believed.]

After Paul finished, he was mocked. Paul left Mars Hill.

LIFE APPLICATION

{Show the cube and the cone.}

When we look at these, no matter what angle we see them from, they are still a cube and a cone. What is different is our perception of what we are seeing.

Paul taught people about Jesus, and even though he might have used different words, he still shared the gospel. These three towns reacted differently to the same truth.

Some in Thessalonica believed, but some Jews became jealous. The two groups heard the same words, the same gospel, and reacted differently.

The Bereans responded to the gospel by searching the Scriptures themselves and seeing the truth of Paul's reasoning. This allowed their knowledge to be stretched and their faith to grow. Therefore, many believed in Jesus. They reacted differently than the Thessalonians.

The Greeks in Athens loved knowledge. They wanted to know many different ideas. They loved logical thinking. The problem with too much logic, or reasoning, is that it does not allow for faith. Paul used logic and reasoning of the Scriptures to present the gospel to them.

The Athenians were so concerned about thinking that they could not grasp the concept of a resurrection. Coming back to life is not logical. It is not supposed to happen. They did not understand that God, who created life, could control death and life.

Is knowledge important? Absolutely! We must learn so we are prepared for whatever type of ministry God wants us to do. But if all we know is facts, even facts about the Bible, then our hearts will not grow in faith. Our hearts will not change. Head knowledge must become heart knowledge.

{Ask:}

- What do you think it means to "turn the world upside down"? [To influence people to begin doing the opposite of what they were doing]

- How were Paul and Silas doing this? [They were teaching the gospel of Christ, and repentance was doing the opposite of what the people, or sinners, were doing.]

- How can you turn the world upside down for God? [Make sure that I have repented of my sins and then go tell others how they can repent as well.]

What can we learn from Paul's messages to these three cities? When the gospel is presented to us, we can respond without thinking, like the jealous Jews. We can respond with only thinking and no faith, like the Athenians. Or we can respond with thought and faith, like the Bereans. Which way do you respond to the gospel?

COMMENT BOX

■ ■ ■ ■ ■ ■ ■ ■ ■ ■ ■ ■ ■ ■ ■ ■ ■ ■ ■

THINK: What went well as you taught this lesson? What can you do better?

_____

_____

_____

_____

_____

_____

_____

_____

TIP: This lesson is another good time to rehearse the gospel with the children. Have a volunteer explain the gospel to everyone, or have the children pair up to practice. Listen to the words used by the children so you can assess how well YOU have explained the gospel. If you need to tweak your teaching, do it.

16 THE SCRAMBLED TIMELINE

■ ■ ■ ■ ■ ■ ■ ■ ■ ■ ■ ■ ■ ■ ■ ■ ■ ■ ■ ■

Paul met many friends throughout his missionary journeys. Use this scrambled timeline activity from Acts 18 to discuss a series of events and the people Paul met along the way.

Scripture Focus: Acts 18

Materials:

- List of Acts 18 events (See the Resource Page to print the list.)
- Paper
- Glue
- Scissors

- Whiteboard (this is what I used)
- Images of Athens, Corinth, Ephesus, Jerusalem, and Antioch from the Resource Page
- Acts 18:5 poster

{Preparation: Draw the timeline on the paper or the board with 20 dashes. Number the events with a small number so you know the order they should be in. Cut apart the timeline events and the pictures. Scramble the information.}

Geography: Athens; Corinth; Syria; Ephesus; Caesarea; Jerusalem; Antioch

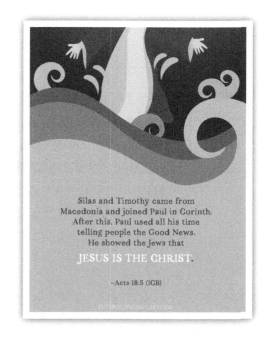

Silas and Timothy came from Macedonia and joined Paul in Corinth. After this, Paul used all his time telling people the Good News. He showed the Jews that

JESUS IS THE CHRIST.

–Acts 18:5 (ICB)

Background: Paul is on his second missionary journey with Silas. Paul went to Lystra and invited Timothy to join them. In Philippi they met Lydia. Paul, Silas, and Timothy went to Thessalonica. Paul and Silas left during the night and went to Berea. Then the Jews from Thessalonica came to town and began to stir up the crowd. The new church sent Paul away by ship. Silas and Timothy stayed behind. Paul traveled to Athens. He told the people that His God had made all of the stone, gold, or silver used to make their gods. Paul explained that God was the Creator of all things. After Paul finished and was mocked, he left Mars Hill.

BIBLE LESSON

■ ■ ■ ■ ■ ■ ■ ■ ■ ■ ■ ■ ■ ■ ■ ■ ■ ■

{This chapter in Acts has many different events that are interesting to read. Cut apart the events and create a timeline as you or the children read Acts 18. I used a white board to create a class timeline and had the kids read the chapter from their Bibles and tell me where to put the info. If you have older children, give them their own timeline pieces to glue onto a sheet of paper.}

{Be sure to have the name of the location on the image. This will help the children understand that the events took place in an actual location.}

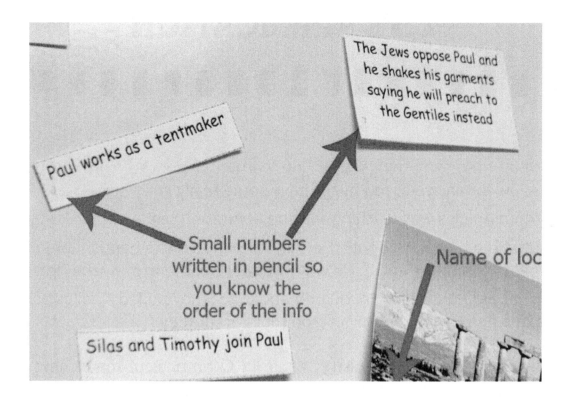

{Read Acts 18 and slowly add the events and images to the timeline. I thought that the 5 to 8-years-olds would have a hard time with this activity. While it was a challenge, they stepped up, dug into their Bibles, and plowed through it beautifully!! I was SO impressed!!}

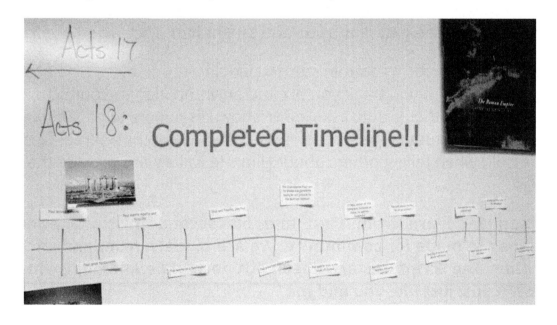

LIFE APPLICATION

██ █ ██ █ ██ █ ██ █ ██ █ ██ █ ██ █ ██ █ ██ █ ██ █ ██ █ ██

{Ask:}

- What interesting things have you learned or noticed from our timeline? [Allow for answers; you might have some really good conversations!]

- When Apollos was teaching, was he accurate? [Yes]

- What did he know about? [He only knew about the baptism of John. This means John the Baptist. He was not aware of baptism by the Holy Spirit.]

- What did Aquila and Priscilla do about it? [They pulled Apollos aside and explained to him the way of God more accurately.]

Friends are important in ministry. While in Corinth, Paul made new friends while waiting for his old friends to arrive. While new friends are great, it was not until Silas and Timothy arrived that Paul began to preach with boldness.

Apollos was another preacher, like Paul, who traveled around preaching about Jesus. He may have been a better speaker than Paul. While Apollos was accurate in his teachings, his knowledge about baptism was not quite complete. Aquila and Priscilla could have denounced the man and argued with his teaching publicly. Instead, they drew Apollos aside and taught him. They acted like friends.

God never intends for us to minister to people on our own. God has "many people in the city." If you think you are the only Christian in your school classroom or in some other group, ask God to show His people to you. It might be a teacher, another student, or someone you have never considered. God wants us to be bold when telling others about Him. He will always provide the people you need.

What can we learn from Paul and his second missionary journey? Christians are made for community. We are to learn from and encourage each other. The Scriptures are filled with normal people doing their best to follow Jesus, just like you and me.

COMMENT BOX

■ ■

THINK: What went well as you taught this lesson? What can you do better?

_____

_____

_____

_____

_____

_____

_____

_____

_____

TIP: You can do a variation of this lesson and have older children pair together and work to create the timeline.

17 GET RID OF THE SIN

This object lesson is based on Acts 19 which took place during the years of Paul's third missionary journey. Teach children to define repentance and to describe the actions of a heart changed by belief in Jesus.

Scripture Focus: Acts 19:11-20

Materials:

- 4 clear/glass bowls
- Water-based paint
- Chocolate syrup
- Crushed crackers or cereal
- Clean water
- Acts 19:20 poster

{Preparation: Put some paint, syrup, crackers, and water in separate bowls. Put enough in each bowl so that you can cover at least half, or more, of your hand. Be able to clean your hand in the water bowl.}

FUTUREFLYINGSAUCERS.COM

In a powerful way
the word of the Lord kept
spreading and growing.

–Acts 19:20 (ICB)

Geography: Antioch; Galatia; Phrygia; Ephesus

Background: Paul completed his second missionary journey and returned to Antioch. After "spending some time there," he began his third journey by traveling back to the cities in Galatia and Phrygia, "strengthening the disciples." While Paul was traveling, a man named Apollos was preaching in the area of Ephesus. He taught about the baptism of John, or a baptism of repentance. Aquila and Priscilla pulled Apollos aside and taught him accurately. Then there was no stopping him! He preached and preached, and he traveled on to Corinth.

BIBLE LESSON

{Read the Scripture or tell the story. This is an amazing event, so be sure to read with enthusiasm. Ask:}

- Who is in this Scripture? [God, Paul, Jewish exorcists, the seven sons of Sceva, the evil spirit, the man with the evil spirit]
- What was God allowing to happen? [During these two years, God allowed many unusual miracles to happen through Paul. People could take handkerchiefs and aprons that belonged to Paul and give them to the sick, diseased, and demon-possessed, and they would be healed.]

Paul stayed in Ephesus for two years, and the Scriptures say that all who dwelt in Asia heard the word.

Some unbelieving Jews decided to get in on the action and use the name of Jesus to cast out demons. There were seven sons of a Jewish leader named Sceva. As they attempted to cast out a demon in a man, the demon responded with, *"Jesus I know. Paul I know. But who are you?"* And the man with the demons attacked the seven brothers until they ran away wounded and naked.

{Ask:}

- What can we learn from the evil spirit? [This tells us that Satan knows who belongs to Jesus and that Jesus is powerful!]

Because of this incident, the people feared the Lord, and Jesus was magnified! Many people who believed in Jesus began to tell about and confess their wrong ways of living. In fact, many of those who practiced witchcraft and magic gathered all of their spell books and made bonfires in the streets of the town.

{Ask:}

- Think about books that were written 2,000 years ago. [Lead the children through a conversation discussing how long it took to get a book written in those days. They did not have printing presses. Their books were handwritten and were very expensive. Only the rich people would have had books.]
- What does the Scripture tell us about these books? [The value of everything burned totaled 50,000 pieces of silver.]

The burning of books was a HUGE deal!

The people did not stop there. They stopped buying the silver shrines that were made in Ephesus. This upset the silversmiths because they were not able to make money if people stopped buying the fake gods. Riots broke out, and people were angry.

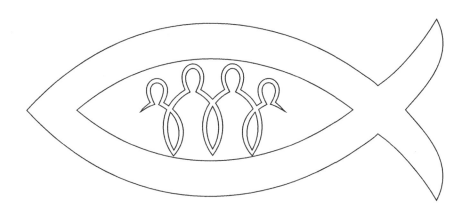

LIFE APPLICATION AND OBJECT LESSON

{Show the four bowls.}

The Bible tells us that we have all sinned. Our grandparents are sinful. Our parents are sinful. Every person ever born on the earth was, and is, sinful. We were born into sin. Sin is anything that we think, say, or do that does not please God.

{Put your hand into the bowl of paint and cover at least all of your fingers.}

As we grow and learn, we do wrong things. We make selfish decisions. Sometimes we are mean to other people. We disobey our parents. We think bad things in our minds.

{Put your hand in the chocolate syrup.}

Sin is messy. It clings to us, and it grows.

{Put your hand in the crushed crackers.}

   • Can my hand clean itself? [No]

{Carefully shake your hand or slide it across the top of a bowl. DO NOT use the water bowl.}

There is nothing my hand can do to clean off all the yucky stuff. There is nothing you or I can do to cleanse ourselves of sin.

The Bible tells us that if we confess Jesus with our mouth, then we will be saved.

{Ask:}

   • Saved from what? [We will be saved from our sins. The Bible also tells us that if we confess our sins, Jesus is faithful and just and will forgive us our sins and purify us, or cleanse us, from all unrighteousness.]
   • What is unrighteousness? [Anything we say, think, or do that goes against God's Law]

- What does it mean to confess? [Confessing is being honest about the wrong done and telling God, and sometimes others, about it.]

This is what the people of Ephesus did. They began to confess their sins. They told of their deeds. The believers in Ephesus burned their books and stopped buying certain items they used to buy. They got rid of so much "stuff" that they messed up their economy!

{Ask:}

- Have you ever stopped doing something that was wrong or could hurt you or someone else? [Allow for answers.]
- Is there something you need to stop doing because it does not please God? [Lead a discussion about activities that might be ok by the world's standards, but not ok by God's. Examples: watching violent movies or video games, teasing children who look or act differently, wearing clothes because they are popular, reading comic books too much and not having quiet Bible reading time, etc.]

Once we believe in Jesus, we need to be sure that every part of our life is pleasing to Him. We need to confess our sins to Him. Jesus is the only One who can make us right before God.

{Put your hand in the clean water and wash it.}

Jesus cleanses us. We cannot do it by ourselves. When we choose to believe in Jesus, we cannot help but repent. Repentance is so much more than just "feeling sorry." **We must have a change of heart.** This means choosing to live for Jesus and NOT living for ourselves. It is fighting against the fleshly desires with the armor of God. We should be protecting ourselves from the lies of this world. It is desiring to do what God wants, and not what we want.

What can we learn from Acts 19? We need to stay focused on Jesus as the Holy Spirit teaches us what is good and pleasing to the Lord. If we mess up and sin (which we will), then we must take action by confessing our sins and then being obedient to the Lord. When we confess our sins and allow God to transform our hearts, God can use it to spread His gospel and glory.

COMMENT BOX

■ ■

THINK: What went well as you taught this lesson? What can you do better?

_____

_____

_____

_____

_____

_____

_____

_____

_____

TIP: Remind the children that, through the power of the Holy Spirit, we have the ability to not become entangled with sin.

18 WHAT DOES DENYING ONESELF MEAN?

■ ■

What does it mean to deny oneself? Use this Bible object lesson about Paul choosing to go to Jerusalem and denying himself so he could obey the Holy Spirit instead.

Scripture Focus: Acts 20:1-38

Materials:

- Your favorite snack, such as cookies, etc., but only have enough for the children and not yourself
- Acts 20:22-23 poster

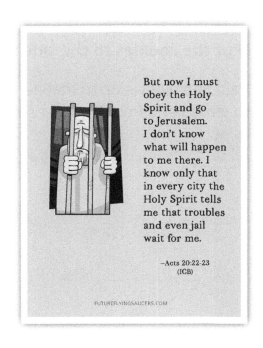

But now I must obey the Holy Spirit and go to Jerusalem. I don't know what will happen to me there. I know only that in every city the Holy Spirit tells me that troubles and even jail wait for me.

–Acts 20:22-23
(ICB)

FUTUREFLYINGSAUCERS.COM

Geography: Ephesus; Macedonia; Greece; back to Macedonia; Philippi; Troas; Assos; Mitylene; Chlos; Samos; Trogyllium; Miletus; back to Ephesus

Paul is ending his third missionary journey. He had traveled from Ephesus into Macedonia and Greece, only to turn around and retrace his steps, knowing that his journey would eventually lead him to Jerusalem.

Background: Paul stayed in Ephesus for two years, and the Scriptures say that all who dwelt in Asia heard the word. Lives were changing so much that the economy was being affected. People were not buying silver idols, and a riot ensued. After the riot in Ephesus calmed down, Paul decided to leave town and visit the churches in Macedonia and Greece, which had been started on his second missionary journey.

OBJECT LESSON

■ ■

{Show the cookies to the children and explain that this is your favorite snack. Describe why you like these particular cookies so much. Then tell them that you have cookies for almost everyone. Tell them that you are one cookie short. Act like you are struggling. Talk through the decision to give all of your favorite cookies away and not take one yourself. What are you feeling? Talk through the temptation of keeping them all to yourself and not sharing any, or maybe leaving one other child out. Ask:}

- Is it always easy to make the right decision? [No]
- What would you do if you were me right now? [Allow for answers. You might get suggestions such as cutting the cookies into halves.]

We could cut the cookies in half and then everyone could at least get something. Maybe we will do that later.

{Put the cookies to the side for now.}

Paul had a decision to make—a tough decision. He knew God wanted him to go to Jerusalem. People in Jerusalem wanted Paul dead. Let's see what he decides to do.

BIBLE LESSON

{Read Acts 20:1-6. Ask:}

- Where did Paul decide to go first? [Macedonia]

- What did he do while he was there? [He encouraged the disciples and churches with encouraging words.]

- How long did he stay in Greece? [Three months]

- What caused Paul to change his travel plans? [The Jews were plotting against him.]

- Sopater was from Berea. Do you remember what made the Bereans special? [After they heard the gospel from Paul, the Bereans searched the Scriptures to see if they agreed with him, and then many believed.]

{Read Acts 20:7-12. Ask:}

- Why do you think this particular event in Paul's ministry is included in the Bible? [Allow for answers. Luke mentions the gathering of believers on the first day of the week. He might have been counting days as a Roman would have because he was a Gentile; the Jews would have counted days from sundown to sundown. This Scripture helps us to see that the church was meeting on Sunday. It is possible that church met at night and that Paul preached until midnight.]

- What happened around midnight? [Eutychus fell out of the window because he fell asleep.]

A young man named Eutychus was sitting in a window on the third floor of this house. He fell asleep and fell out of the window and died. Paul raced down the stairs and embraced the young man, and he came back to life. Paul returned upstairs, ate, and taught until morning.

{Read Acts 20:17-23, 36-38.}

The men traveled to Miletus, which is just south of Ephesus. Paul called for the elders of Ephesus to come down to him. They came, and Paul began to share his BAD NEWS with them. He told the men that the Holy Spirit was telling him to travel to Jerusalem and that afflictions awaited him there.

Paul reassured them that it was OK. He said that his life belonged to Jesus. There was more BAD NEWS. Paul told the men that they would never see his face again. He told them to be watchful and to be on guard because men were going to rise up and try to teach wrong things about Jesus.

{Hold up the cookies.}

- Are cookies really all that important? [Allow for answers. No.]
- Let's read verses 36-38 again. Why were the elders filled with sorrow? [They knew they would never see Paul again; they knew he was going to die.]
- Do you think Paul struggled to tell the men he would be going to Jerusalem and would not see them again? [Yes]
- Did we struggle over the lack of cookies? [Yes]
- How did Paul know he had to go? [He was bound in the spirit and listening to the Holy Spirit.]
- If you are a believer of Jesus, do you have the same Holy Spirit inside of you? [Yes]

Paul exhorted the elders to study the Word of God and to care for those who were needy and weak. The people listening to Paul began to weep. They embraced Paul and took him to his ship.

LIFE APPLICATION

{Ask:}

- Can you say you are ready to die for Jesus if He asked you to? [Allow for answers. It will probably be quiet.]

{Hold up the cookies.}

Dying for Jesus doesn't necessarily mean physically dying for Him, although it could. Dying to self means giving up something that means a lot to us for the good of Jesus or someone else. Paul knew he had to obey the Holy Spirit; in doing that, he was dying to self, or doing what is called denying himself.

These cookies are my favorite. But I am one short.

I want you to have them. At the end of this lesson, I am going to give all of you one cookie. I will deny what I want so you can have something good. We could have split these in half so I could have had something. If I had done that, then I would not have had the opportunity to fully bless you with these cookies.

Denying myself of a favorite cookie is a little thing.

{Ask:}

- What is an example of denying ourselves, or dying to ourselves, when it comes to our family and friends? [Allow for answers. Examples could include doing a brother's chore to help him out even when you do not want to; buying a specific toy you want and giving it away to a friend for a birthday present; helping someone who might look different; etc.]

Sometimes dying to self means looking at how you live your life and seeing if there is anything you do that is more important than God's work. The Holy Spirit can help you to see what is distracting you from serving God and growing in Jesus. That might mean choosing to not do something OR choosing to do something that is hard to do. It might mean doing the thing your heart might not want to do. It might mean giving up what you cherish the most. Dying to self means cutting sin out of your life. It means actually walking the walk of

Jesus and not just talking about it. It means doing the right thing even when it might hurt.

{Give each of the children a cookie and do not give one to yourself. Watch their reactions.}

What can we learn from Paul in Acts 20? If you say you are a Christian, that means you must recognize the fact that your life is not your own. It was bought by God when Jesus died on that cross. You are His. Paul recognized this, and he is a great example of dying to self, or self-denial. He had a life that was broken and spilled out for Jesus.

COMMENT BOX

■ ■ ■ ■ ■ ■ ■ ■ ■ ■ ■ ■ ■ ■ ■ ■ ■ ■ ■

THINK: What went well as you taught this lesson? What can you do better?

_____

_____

_____

_____

_____

_____

_____

_____

TIP: "Churchy" words can be hard for children to understand. Use stories from your own life to exemplify ideas such as confession, repentance, self-denial, righteousness, and salvation.

19 HOW TO SHARE YOUR TESTIMONY

■ ■

What is a testimony? How do you get one? What should you do with it? Discuss these questions and more with this Bible activity lesson about Paul in Jerusalem.

Scripture Focus: Acts 21:15-22:30

Materials:

- Construction paper (two sheets of the same color, and one sheet that is red)
- (Optional) Make sign sets for each child by creating the signs above in a smaller format and taping them onto Popsicle sticks.
- Acts 22:15-16 Poster

Geography: Caesarea; Jerusalem

Background: Paul's third missionary journey was over, and he followed the prompting of the Holy Spirit to go to Jerusalem, knowing that trials awaited him. He visited Herod's Temple, which was the same temple Jesus visited. When Paul was younger, he studied under the Pharisee named Gamaliel.

"You will be his witness to all people. You will tell them about the things you have seen and heard. Now, why wait any longer? Get up, be baptized, and wash your sins away. Do this, trusting in him to save you."

-Acts 22:15-16 (ICB)

FUTUREFLYINGSAUCERS.COM

ACTIVITY LESSON

■ ■ ■ ■ ■ ■ ■ ■ ■ ■ ■ ■ ■ ■ ■ ■ ■ ■ ■ ■

{Cut the shape of a cross out of the red sheet of paper. On the other sheets of paper, write the word BEFORE on one and the word AFTER on the other.}

{Ask:}

- What is a testimony? [Allow for answers. Discuss a court case and how the witnesses give their testimonies. They share what they saw happen. Therefore, whenever a person talks about their personal experience with something, they are sharing their testimony.]

Everyone who chooses to believe in Jesus has a testimony, or a "Jesus Story." Every story is different.

{Show the BEFORE sign.}

Before people meet Jesus, they are one way.

{Show the cross. Put it to the right of the BEFORE sign.}

When people choose to follow Jesus, there is a spiritual change inside of them. There are ways people in the church describe this. Maybe you have heard of people transforming from darkness to light. Other examples include: the old man to the new man, unrighteousness to righteousness, or not saved from sin to saved from sin. Those are different ways to explain the same process.

{Show the AFTER sign. Put it on the right side of the cross.}

After this spiritual change takes place, a person is...just that, changed. Behaviors change. Habits change. Actions change. These changes do not necessarily happen fast. They may take years to change. However, after a person meets Jesus and decides to follow Him, life looks different. They focus on God being their Master instead of them being their own master.

BIBLE LESSON

Paul has a great example of a testimony.

{Show the three signs. Choose three children. Give one sign to each. Explain:}

As we learn Paul's testimony, when we hear about Paul BEFORE Jesus, let's lift up the BEFORE sign. When we hear about Paul meeting Jesus, hold up the cross. When we hear about how Paul changed, hold up the AFTER sign.

{Read Acts 21:26-40. Depending upon the age of the children, you might want to tell this part of the event and read only Paul's testimony. Ask:}

- Where did Paul go? [Into the temple]
- With whom? [Four Jewish brethren who were ending their time of vows]

These vows were probably Nazirite vows, which Jews would take periodically for different reasons. Some examples of people with Nazirite vows from Scripture would be Samson, Samuel, and John the Baptist. During their time of vow, the Jews would not drink anything from grapes and would not cut their hair. Paul was supposed to go with these men and pay for them to have their heads shaven. Doing this would show the temple leaders that the vows were complete and that Paul really did still abide by the Jewish customs.

{Ask:}

- Did Paul's plan work? [No]
- Who stirred up trouble? [A handful of Jews from Asia]
- Of what did they accuse Paul? [Teaching all men to be against the Jews and allowing Greeks into the temple to defile it]
- What happened? [The men grabbed Paul, all the city was disturbed, they dragged him out of the temple, and the doors were shut.]

While the Jews were seeking to kill Paul, the commander of the garrison heard about the uproar. The commander and some soldiers immediately went to the area. They stopped the beating of Paul. They placed him in two chains and asked the crowd who this was and what he had done. There were conflicting answers. The commander could not figure out the truth, so he started to take Paul to the barracks. When they got to the stairs, soldiers had to carry Paul because of what the mob had done to him. As Paul was leaving, the crowd began to say, *"Away with him!"*

{Ask:}

- Do you remember learning something special about Paul when he was arrested before? [Paul was a Roman citizen.]

Paul would not have missed the gravity of this moment. The soldiers were taking him to the Antonia Fortress, which is across the Court of the Gentiles from Herod's Temple. The staircase that the soldiers were using would take Paul up to the very platform where Pilate presented Jesus to the multitude.

Paul asked the commander if he could speak to the crowd.

{Read Acts 22:1-21. Use the signs during this Scripture section.}

Paul told his story. When he got to the part about Jesus telling him to go to the Gentiles, the mob began to yell and scream. The commander ordered Paul to be brought into the barracks and whipped. Paul explained to the commander that he was born a Roman.

{Ask:}

- How did the centurion become a Roman? [He paid a large sum of money.]

Immediately Paul was unbound, but the commander still wanted to understand what was going on. He released Paul but commanded the chief priests and the council to appear before him. Paul was to stand before them.

Thus the trials began.

LIFE APPLICATION

It is quite possible that Paul literally stood in the footsteps of Jesus. Paul knew that suffering was going to take place in Jerusalem. He went anyway, and he went boldly in the Lord. He knew who he was. He knew the calling God had placed on his life, and he was not ashamed. He shared his testimony in front of everyone in the temple.

{Ask:}

- What was Paul like before Jesus? [Allow for answers.]
- What did Paul do after he met Jesus? [Allow for answers.]

{The children you are teaching may or may not have a "Jesus Story," or testimony. Be sensitive to those who may not have chosen to follow Jesus yet. Consider sharing the gospel with them. Share a short version of your testimony. As you do, hold up the signs BEFORE, the CROSS, and AFTER describing how your life changed because of Jesus. Ask:}

- Can you think of another person from the Bible who has a testimony? [Allow for answers. Consider the disciples, Stephen, Lydia, Timothy, the centurion after the earthquake, etc.]

{Choose the centurion and review his story while holding up the signs. His testimony is different because he didn't physically meet Jesus, but he heard the gospel and knew he needed to repent. Ask:}

- What about you? If you have a testimony, are you willing to share it? [Allow for children to tell their stories. This will give you an opportunity to look into their spiritual world to see how much they understand about following Jesus.]
- What should we do with our Jesus Story? [Tell other people how Jesus has changed us and is changing us]

What can we learn from Paul telling his testimony? Paul was always ready to tell how Jesus had changed his life. He was not ashamed of his background, and he knew that Jesus had transformed him into a new man. If you have a Jesus Story, then you have had a new beginning as well. You are not walking in darkness anymore—you are in God's light!

COMMENT BOX

■ ■ ■ ■ ■ ■ ■ ■ ■ ■ ■ ■ ■ ■ ■ ■ ■ ■

THINK: What went well as you taught this lesson? What can you do better?

_____

_____

_____

_____

_____

_____

_____

_____

_____

TIP: This is a good lesson to use to assess your students' understanding of salvation and life change. Use what you learn to critique your teaching. Write your thoughts on the lines above.

20 THE INSIDE MATTERS

■ ■

Both Jesus and Paul called the Jewish leaders whitewashed tombs, or walls. Why should we care? Use this Bible science lesson from Acts 23 to discuss the beginning of Paul's trials before governing authorities.

Scripture Focus: Acts 23:1-11

Materials:

- Tarp or plastic table cloth
- Metal pie pan or cookie sheet
- Sand
- 4 tsp. granulated sugar
- 1 tsp. baking soda
- Rubbing alcohol
- Lighter
- Plastic cup
- Fire extinguisher (just in case!)
- Acts 23:11 poster

{Preparation: This is a chemical reaction involving fire. Therefore, you will want to do this outside. Put the tarp on the ground or on the table. Fill the pie pan with the sand. Flatten the sand. Put baking soda and sugar in the plastic cup.}

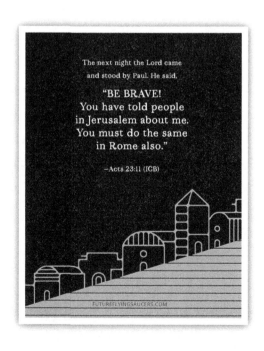

The next night the Lord came and stood by Paul. He said,

"BE BRAVE! You have told people in Jerusalem about me. You must do the same in Rome also."

—Acts 23:11 (ICB)

FUTUREFLYINGSAUCERS.COM

Geography: Jerusalem; Caesarea

Background: Review is important for this lesson, or meaning will be lost. Remember, before Paul met Jesus on the road to Damascus, he was a Jewish Pharisee. Paul was persecuting people of The Way. Paul had the blessings and backing of the Jewish Council. The Pharisees and Sadducees were always at odds with each other. Pharisees believed in angels, spirits, and the possibility of resurrection of the dead; the Sadducees did not believe in any of that.

While Jesus was on earth, He pointed out that the belief system of those leaders was dead wrong. Jesus even verbally accused some of the leaders of being whitewashed tombs. They were clean on the outside and dead on the inside.

OBJECT AND BIBLE LESSON

■ ■

{Set the pie tin in front of you. Make sure the children are far enough away so they will not put fingers in the fire. Read Acts 23:1-11.}

Paul is in a strange situation. The Jewish leaders want Paul arrested so they can try him and possibly kill him. The Romans have Paul in custody for his protection.

{Ask:}

- What happened after Paul spoke one sentence? [The high priest struck him.]

- How did Paul respond? [He called the high priest a whitewashed wall and said that he, Paul, was being unjustly struck.]

- Did Paul realize it was the high priest who struck him? [Allow for answers. Commentaries vary on this. Perhaps Paul did not know who was high priest at this time because he had been away traveling for 20 years. Another opinion states that Paul jokingly or sarcastically responded that he did not recognize the high priest because a true high priest would be a different type of person.]

Ananias, who was the high priest at this time, was a political leader rather than a spiritual one. The books of Exodus and Leviticus give us great information about the type of man God wanted as high priest of the Jews.

{Ask:}

- What are the differences between the Sadducees and the Pharisees? [The Sadducees claim there is no such thing as resurrection, angels, or spirit; the Pharisees do believe in those things.]

Ananias was a Sadducee, which meant he did not believe in a spirit. God is Spirit (John 4:24). It is sad to think that he was the high priest. Once a year Ananias would go into the Holiest of Holies to make atonement for his nation. It is possible Ananias might not have even believed in God.

Aaron, Moses' brother, was the first high priest. The position and title were supposed to be carried down from father to son. However, after the exile, the position of high priest became more of a political office. The high priest was chosen by Rome.

Ananias, the high priest, was known to be a vicious and violent man.

{Ask:}

- Do you think Paul was correct in calling the high priest a whitewashed wall? [Allow for answers.]
- What does it mean to be whitewashed? [Allow for answers. Whitewash is a white paint used on walls to hide imperfections.]
- Jesus called the Jewish leaders whitewashed tombs. What do you think that meant? [The tombs look white and nice on the outside, but there are dead bones on the inside of the tomb.]

{Hold up the cup of sugar and baking soda.}

This is sugar and baking soda. It is pure sugar and pure baking soda. There is no dirt or anything in it.

{Take the alcohol and pour some on the sand, making a pool about 5-6 inches in diameter in the middle of the pan.}

The Bible tells us that when Jesus judges us in heaven, our deeds will be burned. Bad deeds will burn away like wood or hay. Good deeds will withstand the fire like gold and precious stones (1 Corinthians 3:10-15).

Let's say that the powder is the high priest and the other Jewish leaders who were attacking Paul. He called them whitewashed walls, similar to whitewashed tombs. White on the outside. Dead on the inside.

{Pour the white mixture on top and in the middle of the alcohol on the sand. Use the lighter to light the alcohol. Wait a few minutes. The sugar should begin to turn black, and a gross-looking (and really neat!) sugar snake should appear. Get ready for a reaction from the children! It will take between 5 and 10 minutes for all of the sugar to burn. As it does, discuss how the black snake looks. Talk about how our hearts are deceitful, and that if we have a yucky heart, then bad actions come out, just like the

Jewish leaders. We would be whitewashed walls that look nice and clean on the outside, but are dirty and filled with ash on the inside. Once the sugar is finished burning, the fire will go out. Wait about 30 seconds or so and then carefully pick up the snake. You can crush it over the sand and show how the entire black snake is carbon ash.}

The Jewish leaders fought among themselves and wanted to tear Paul apart. Therefore, the Romans took Paul back into the jail.

That night the Lord stood by Paul. (How awesome and encouraging is that?!?) The Lord told Paul to be of good cheer and that he would be going to Rome.

LIFE APPLICATION

■ ■ ■ ■ ■ ■ ■ ■ ■ ■ ■ ■ ■ ■ ■ ■ ■ ■ ■ ■

"Be of good cheer!" the Lord told Paul. Be of good cheer? He was being falsely accused, people wanted him dead, he was locked in a jail, and he was not getting to spread the gospel as Jesus had told him to. We must remember that God's ways are not our ways. Many trials we face are for the explicit purpose of "getting us to Rome," so that God can get us to a point in life where He can further His gospel through us.

God wants His people to have pure hearts and pure motives. He does not want whitewashed tombs.

{Ask:}

- Think of those black snakes. What type of actions, attitudes, habits, or words come out of your heart? [Allow for answers. Lead children into a time of repentance.]

- Do you need to ask God to forgive you for something? [Allow for a time of prayer.]

Maybe you are going through a trial now that will allow you to be a "witness in Rome." Maybe it will allow you to reach people for Jesus who would not have heard the gospel if you had not gone through the trial. Perhaps God is dealing with some yucky sin in your heart before He has you do a good work.

What can we learn from Paul and the Jewish leaders? Be of good cheer! If the Holy Spirit is convicting you of sin in your life, then listen to Him! He wants you pure on the inside so you can do good works that will last for eternity. God wants you to spread His gospel and be His witness.

COMMENT BOX

■ ■ ■ ■ ■ ■ ■ ■ ■ ■ ■ ■ ■ ■ ■ ■ ■ ■ ■ ■

THINK: What went well as you taught this lesson? What can you do better?

_____

_____

_____

_____

_____

_____

_____

_____

_____

TIP: You can add a discussion to this lesson. Ask the children if they know the "jobs" of the Holy Spirit. Once you get some answers, explain that one of the things the Holy Spirit will do is help us know right from wrong. He will help us make good choices that will reflect God.

21 PAUL AND KING AGRIPPA

■ ■

Play a simple game to discuss the art of persuasion as you teach this Bible lesson about Paul almost persuading King Agrippa.

Scripture Focus: Acts 25:13-22, 26:19-23

Materials:

- Index cards
- Acts 26:29 poster

{Preparation: Write simple truths on 5-6 index cards, depending upon the number of children you have. Examples: 2+2=4; a cat has fur; rain falls down and not up; the sky is blue; gravity exists. If you have younger children, use simpler facts; if you have older ones, use more complex facts.}

Geography: Caesarea

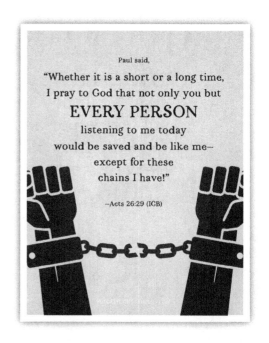

Paul said,

"Whether it is a short or a long time, I pray to God that not only you but **EVERY PERSON** listening to me today would be saved and be like me— except for these chains I have!"

—Acts 26:29 (ICB)

Background: It is important to remember of what the Jewish leaders originally accused Paul. They had accused him of teaching all men to be against the Jews. They had also accused him of defiling the temple by bringing a Gentile into an area where Gentiles were not supposed to be. Of course, both accusations were incorrect.

Knowing some history is important as well. There are three Roman governors mentioned in the New Testament: Pontius Pilate, Felix, and Festus. Being leaders of the Holy Land meant that Felix and Festus were familiar with Jewish customs and beliefs. They would also have been knowledgeable of how volatile the region was. They would have been motivated to keep the Jews happy so that no fighting would break out. King Agrippa was the great-grandson of King Herod (who had had the babies of Bethlehem slaughtered). Agrippa was a practicing Jew and was very familiar with the Scriptures. Bernice was his sister. At this time in the early years of his reign, Caesar Nero was known as a relatively good leader of Rome.

OBJECT LESSON

■ ■ ■ ■ ■ ■ ■ ■ ■ ■ ■ ■ ■ ■ ■ ■ ■ ■ ■ ■

{Choose child volunteers and give each one a card. Be sure to give cards to children who can handle proving the existence of that fact.}

I have given you a card with a fact on it. You need to read that fact and think about it. When it is your turn, you need to convince me that your fact is true. You are going to try to persuade me to believe you.

{Have the first child read the fact. Say in a questioning manner, "I do not think that is true. Persuade me." Allow for rational arguments using math, science, and evidence. For 2+2=4, the child might say, "It just is." Respond with, "Prove it. Persuade me to believe you." Then they might think through finding four objects, holding up one at a time and saying something such as, "Two objects and add another two objects, etc." to prove that 2+2=4. Agree with them and then move on the next fact. Be silly with this process and come up with crazy arguments such as, "No, 2+2 really equals 5." Don't be so difficult that you frustrate the children. You might need to lead some of the children with questions.}

BIBLE LESSON

■ ■ ■ ■ ■ ■ ■ ■ ■ ■ ■ ■ ■ ■ ■ ■ ■ ■ ■ ■

Paul was in jail in Caesarea. He had been there for two years. Governor Felix, who had put Paul there after the Jewish leaders fought over him, was no longer in power. Governor Festus had taken his place. When Festus took over, the high priest told Festus how he wanted Paul to come back to Jerusalem. (Of course, he did not tell Festus he wanted Paul ambushed and killed on the way!) After ten days, Festus had a trial for Paul. The high priest and leaders complained about Paul, but they did not have enough proof to bring charges against him. Festus asked Paul, *"Are you willing to stand trial in Jerusalem?"* Paul responded, *"To the Jews I have done no wrong. I appeal to Caesar."* In response Festus said, *"You appeal to Caesar? To Caesar you shall go!"*

{Read Acts 25:13-22. Ask:}

- To whom was Governor Festus talking? [King Agrippa, also known as Herod Agrippa]
- Did the Jewish leaders have any real accusations against Paul? [No]
- How did King Agrippa respond to Festus? [He wanted to hear from Paul.]

King Agrippa and his sister Bernice had come to visit. Festus told Agrippa about his Paul problem. Paul was brought before them in chains, and the leaders were in full pomp and circumstance with many other important people. Agrippa said, *"Speak for yourself,"* and Paul started telling his testimony including his conversion, preaching to the Gentiles, and about Jesus being risen from the dead.

{Read Acts 26:19-32. Ask:}

- What did Paul say he was not disobedient to? [The heavenly vision]
- What vision was that? [Paul's vision when he was on his way to Damascus]
- Where had Paul proclaimed the gospel? [Damascus, Jerusalem, Judea, and to the Gentiles]
- How did Governor Festus react to Paul? [He said Paul was insane from learning too much.]
- How did Paul respond? [He said he was not insane, but spoke words of truth and reason.]

- What did Paul know about King Agrippa? [Paul asked him if he believed the prophets and then stated that he knew the king believed them.]

This is a very important question because Agrippa was a Jew. A good Jew believed the prophets. HOWEVER, after the message Paul had just given, if Agrippa stated he believed the prophets, then he would be stating that Jesus was the One who fulfilled them.

- What did King Agrippa tell Paul? [*"You almost persuaded me to be a Christian."*]

Paul so much wanted the king and the others in the room to become believers of Jesus. Paul was taken away, and Agrippa turned to Festus and said, *"This man has done nothing. He would be free if he had not appealed to Caesar."*

LIFE APPLICATION

No one knows who, if anyone, came to know Jesus that day. Paul's testimony was important. He was preaching truth to kings and governors just as Jesus had said he would. He was also on his way to Rome to see Caesar just as Jesus said he would. God's promises are true and trustworthy.

{Hold up the cards, or point to the children who tried to persuade you.}

These are facts that we know to be true. We pretended that you had to persuade me to believe that the facts were true.

Paul stated the facts of the gospel, and King Agrippa was almost persuaded to believe.

The fact of Jesus' resurrection is still a stumbling block to many people. People have a hard time accepting anyone coming back to life. Christianity is THE only religion whose "prophet" or "messiah" is alive. That is why our celebration of Easter is so important. Without Easter, Christmas loses its meaning.

It is your job as a Christian to tell other people the facts about Jesus: how He changed your life, and how the Holy Spirit works in your life now. It is God's job to work in the hearts of people and bring them to repentance and salvation. We present the facts. We attempt to persuade like Paul, but God is the One who changes hearts.

- Is there someone to whom you can tell the facts about Jesus? [Allow for answers. Write down the names of the people and begin praying for them by name that God would change their hearts.]

What can we learn from Paul in Acts 26? We can have the boldness to stand firm and talk about Jesus to people even if they choose to ignore us or think we are insane. Asking God to work in the hearts of other people so that they decide to choose Jesus is so important!

COMMENT BOX

■ ■ ■ ■ ■ ■ ■ ■ ■ ■ ■ ■ ■ ■ ■ ■ ■ ■ ■

THINK: What went well as you taught this lesson? What can you do better?

_____

_____

_____

_____

_____

_____

_____

_____

_____

TIP: Humor is always a good thing to add to a Bible lesson. A touch of silliness can go a long way!

22 SHIPWRECKED!

■ ■

Are we standing on the promises of God? Use this Bible object lesson about Paul being shipwrecked to discuss how God will do what He says He will do.

Scripture Focus: Acts 27

Materials:

- 4-6 full-size cans of soda, half regular and half diet, such as Coke and Diet Coke (Hopefully you can find individual cans of soda. I ended up having to buy six-packs of soda which caused this lesson to be a little more expensive then I wanted it to be. I do not know if this will work with plastic bottles of soda.)
- Large glass bowl
- Water
- Acts 27:25 poster

Geography: Caesarea; Sidon; Myra; Crete; Lasea

Background: Either in a vision or by physically standing beside Paul, Jesus told Paul he would go to Rome. After three trials, Paul appealed to Caesar, so he had to go to Rome.

FUTUREFLYINGSAUCERS.COM

So men, be cheerful!
I trust in God.
Everything will happen
as his angel told me.

—Acts 27:25 (ICB)

OBJECT LESSON

■ ■

{Fill the glass bowl 2/3 full with water. Have the soda cans in no particular order beside the bowl. Ask:}

- What do you think will happen if we put the cans in the bowl of water? [Allow for answers.]

{Carefully place a regular soda in the bowl. It should sink and stand upright in the bowl. Then place a diet drink in the bowl. It should turn slightly sideways and float a little. Do this again with the others. See if the children can figure out which cans are sinking, which are floating, and why. The regular soda cans should sink while the diet cans of soda should float. Regular soda is made of sugar, which is heavier than the ingredients used to sweeten diet sodas. Therefore, cans of regular soda will sink in a bowl of water.}

BIBLE LESSON

{Ask:}

- What is large, floats in water, but can sink during a bad storm? [A ship]

{This is an exciting event with a lot of details. When the Scripture mentions wind or waves, have the children sway back and forth in their seats or pretend to row with oars. When it describes setting sail or throwing items overboard, have the children pretend to do what the Scripture describes. Read Acts 27: 1-8. Ask:}

- What was the name of the centurion and what do we know about him? [Paul was taken to a centurion named Julius of the Augustan, or Imperial, Regiment. He was kind to Paul, and when they put into port, he allowed Paul to see friends and receive care from them.]
- What was the destination of Paul? [Italy]
- Who was with Paul on the ship? [We do not know the specific number of those who traveled with Paul, but we know that Luke, who wrote the books of Luke and Acts, accompanied him, as well as Aristarchus.]

{Read Acts 27:9-44. Have the children act out the adventure.}

- What did Paul advise? [He said that sailing was too dangerous and that he thought the voyage would end in disaster.]
- To whom did the centurion listen? [The centurion listened to the ship's owner instead, who said that Crete was not a good place to spend the winter and that they should press on.]

They set sail, and a tempest took over the ship. They stopped trying to steer and allowed the ship to go as it willed. On the third day of the storm, the sailors lightened the load by getting rid of anything with weight that was not important. Many days passed without seeing the sun or stars. At this point, the sailors and everyone else on the ship began to lose hope. (Remember! Paul IS going to get to Rome! Jesus said so!)

{Ask:}

- What does Paul tell the people? [He said they should have listened to him, but now they should take heart. No one would die because an angel of the Lord had told him so. However, they would run aground and be shipwrecked on an island.]
- How many days went by? [14 days]

The sailors sensed that they were close to land and attempted to sneak off the ship. Paul told the centurion that if he wanted to be saved, then ALL of the men had to stay on the boat. The men were very hungry because they had been saving the food just in case they needed it later. Paul encouraged them to go ahead and eat their fill since no one was going to die. Paul blessed the bread and passed it around to everyone.

{Ask:}

- How many people were on the ship? [276 people]

Everyone ate and then they tossed everything loose and heavy into the ocean.

In the morning they saw land and a bay area! The ship's leadership planned to run the ship into the ground to get out of the storm and get people to land. As they were in the process of getting the ship close enough to the beach, it became stuck too far out, and the violence of the waves began to break the ship apart. The soldiers on the ship were going to kill all of the prisoners. The centurion wanted to save Paul, so he did not allow the killing to happen. Instead, he told everyone, *"If you can swim, jump ship and go to shore. If you cannot swim, float on boards."* Everyone, all 276 people, made it to land. They were on a beach on the island of Malta.

LIFE APPLICATION

Jesus had told Paul that he would go to Rome. Jesus is trustworthy. Therefore, Paul knew, despite the storm and shipwreck, that he would get to Rome.

God has told you things that will happen as well. There are a lot of them. Some promises He has already fulfilled. For example: Israel forming a nation; Jerusalem being destroyed (a few times); and the Messiah's coming from Bethlehem. Some promises have not happened yet, such as Jesus returning to earth. But there are other promises in Scripture that we can claim everyday if we are willing to.

{You might want to have the children look up these Scriptures and highlight them in their Bibles. Ask:}

- Did you know that God has a plan for you? (Jeremiah 29:11)
- Did you know that God gives rest to the weary and power to the weak? (Matthew 11:28, Isaiah 40:28-29, Romans 8:26)
- Did you know God will supply all of your needs? (Philippians 4:19)
- Did you know that NOTHING can separate you from God's love? (Romans 8:38-39)
- Did you now that Jesus sent a Helper to guide you? (John 14:26, John 16:13)
- If you believe in Jesus and follow Him, did you know you are a child of God? (Romans 8:16)
- Did you know that God gives you a spirit of power, love, and self-control? (2 Timothy 1:7)

There are SO many promises that God gives us. Many of them He gives because of His mercy and grace. Others have conditions, such as Proverbs 1:33: *"But all who listen to me will live in peace, untroubled by fear of harm."*

{Ask:}

- What is the condition in this verse? [Listen to God]

- If we do, what will happen? [We will live in peace and untroubled by fear of harm.]

- Does this verse mean bad things will not happen to us? [No, but if we listen to God and are guided by the Holy Spirit, we can still have peace that passes understanding and have no fear, even when bad times come our way.]

What can we learn from Paul and the shipwreck? God is trustworthy and deserves our praise. Which promise of God do you need right now? God says He will do what He says He will do. Search those promises out and claim them by praying them!!

COMMENT BOX

■ ■

THINK: What went well as you taught this lesson? What can you do better?

_____

_____

_____

_____

_____

_____

_____

_____

TIP: Allow the children to move and interact with the telling of the Bible story; it will help them remember the truth of the story. The more learning styles you can include in your teaching, the more ways their brains can connect to what you are doing.

23 PAUL IN MALTA

■ ■

Christians are called to spread the gospel, but the enemy likes to seek and destroy. Use this object lesson about Paul in Malta to discuss why we need to know Scripture and how we can use it to help us share the hope of Jesus.

Scripture Focus: Acts 28

Materials:

- Rubber or stuffed snake (If you have children who enjoy learning about snakes, find a few pictures to show different types of snakes so you can discuss the differences between them.)
- Acts 28:28 poster

Geography: Malta; Italy; Rome; Mediterranean Sea

Background: Either in a vision or by physically standing beside Paul, Jesus told Paul he would go to Rome. Paul appealed to Caesar, and after two years and three trials, he was on his way to Rome. Paul was shipwrecked, but he knew he would make it to Rome. He had no doubts.

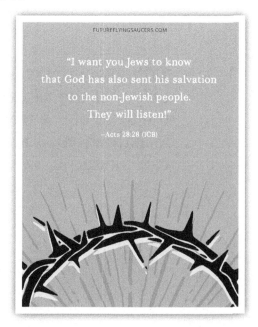

FUTUREFLYINGSAUCERS.COM

"I want you Jews to know that God has also sent his salvation to the non-Jewish people. They will listen!"

—Acts 28:28 (ICB)

OBJECT AND BIBLE LESSON

■ ■

{Show the snake to the children. Ask:}

- How can you tell the difference between a poisonous and nonpoisonous snake? [Allow for answers. There are four main ways: (1) Consider the environment. Some poisonous snakes live in or near ponds and swamps. (2) Look at the coloring of the snake; look especially for yellow and red patterns. (3) Look at the head shape. Poisonous snakes have triangular heads, while non-poisonous snakes have rounded heads. Some nonvenomous snakes like to mimic venomous ones, though, by flattening out their heads. (4) If close enough, examine their eyes. The pupils of a poisonous snake are thin, black, and vertical. Nonpoisonous snakes have round pupils.]

{Use storytelling or read Acts 28:1-10. Ask:}

- Where did Paul and the others land? [The island of Malta]
- How did the people accept them? [The people on the island of Malta were kind to the shipwrecked people.]

The Bible calls these people *natives*. Do not think about a primitive people group. In this case, *native* is the term used for people who had not taken on Greek culture.

{Ask:}

- What kind of weather was it? [It was cold and rainy, but the natives built a fire, and Paul helped.]
- What happened when Paul picked up sticks? [A viper bit Paul on the hand.]
- What type of animal is a snake? [A snake is a reptile. Remind the children that reptiles like warmth and are stiff when the atmosphere is cold; therefore, picking the snake up with sticks definitely could have happened.]

- Why did the natives watch Paul so carefully? [They knew he must be a murderer and was receiving his punishment! A man would swell up and die after being bit by that viper!]

They watched Paul...they watched Paul...they watched Paul...and he did not die.

{Ask:}

- When Paul did not die, what did the natives think? [At this point, the natives changed their opinion and declared Paul to be a god.]

Scripture does not tell us what Paul told the natives. Presumably his reply would have been similar to what he told the people who claimed that he and Barnabas were gods. Paul and Barnabas told the people they were regular men like them.

Paul and the other travelers stayed with a man named Publius for three days. While with him, Paul healed Publius' father. Once people heard the news, everyone on the island who was sick came to see Paul for healing.

After three months, the shipwrecked men boarded a ship and set sail. When Paul got to the Market of Appius, some Christians from Rome met him there and encouraged him. Paul then traveled north on the Appian Way toward Rome. While Paul was imprisoned in Rome, he was allowed to rent his own house, and he had one guard watching over him. During this time of imprisonment, Paul wrote the letters of Philemon, Ephesians, Colossians, and Philippians.

{Read Acts 28:23-31. Ask:}

- With whom did Paul meet? [The Jewish people]

Paul called all the Jewish leadership to his home and explained the prophets, Jesus, and the Scripture prophecies and fulfillments. Some were persuaded, but others were not. Paul stated once again that he would preach to the Gentiles because of the unbelief of the Jews.

Paul was imprisoned for two years. During those two years he preached and taught anyone who came to him. Paul's letters to Timothy and to Titus tell us that Paul was released from prison in Rome. Then Scripture is almost silent as to what happened to Paul. Some scholars think Paul might have journeyed to

Spain because of some of his comments in his letters. At some point, he was imprisoned again. Nero was the Caesar at this time, and persecution of Christians became the norm. *Foxe's Book of Martyrs* says that Paul was beheaded outside the city, but there does not seem to be any documentation of his death.

Thanks to Paul's service and obedience to the Lord, the gospel spread and expanded throughout the world.

LIFE APPLICATION

■ ■

{Show the toy snake. Ask:}

- Why should we know about snakes? [Allow for answers. It is important for us to know about snakes that live in our area so we can react properly if we see one.]

- Why is it important for us to know what is in the Bible? [Allow for answers. Discuss that knowing the Scripture will help us to know what is true, and what is not, in a confusing world.]

- Can you think of another time when snakes are seen in the Scriptures? [Allow for answers. Examples include the Fall in the garden; Moses throwing down his rod which turned into a snake and ate the snakes of Pharaoh's magicians; in the desert, poisonous snakes came into the Israelite camp and bit the people.]

Many times, snakes are seen as the enemy because Satan took on the form of a snake-like creature. Satan is the enemy of God. Paul, a man of God, was bitten by a snake, but was able to shake it off and continue with what he was doing.

{Ask:}

- Did you know that Satan is still the enemy of God? [Yes]

- What does Satan try to do? [Allow for answers, but lead the children to understand that Satan wants to seek and devour like an angry, hungry lion (1 Peter 5:8).]

- Do you remember what Jesus did to fight Satan in the wilderness? [He used Scripture.]

- What can you do to fight off Satan when he tries to lie to you? [Use Scripture to tell yourself the truth.]

Paul taught the Scriptures, and he taught about the kingdom of God to whomever would listen to him. Some believed, and some did not. You have been taught from the Scriptures by your mom and dad or by the church. You have that same choice. You can believe the gospel of Jesus, or not.

{Ask:}

- What is the gospel of Jesus? [Allow for answers. Be sure that they explain something like this: (1) God is holy. (2) People are sinful. (3) God sent Jesus to the earth. (4) Jesus was sinless and died on the cross. (5) When Jesus died and rose again, he took all of your sins on Himself. (6) Because of this, through belief in Jesus Christ, we can be righteous before God. (7) If you believe in Jesus and choose to follow Him, then He is your Master and you do what He commands with your life. If the children cannot explain the gospel to you, then this is a sign that they need to rehearse sharing the gospel.]

What can we learn from Paul in Malta? Like Paul, we are to share the gospel with whomever will listen to us. However, there will be times when Satan, our enemy, will try to seek and destroy what we are trying to do for God. He likes to mess up our relationships with people. He likes to frustrate us. We can be like Paul and know the Scriptures well enough to "toss the serpent of Satan into the fire" and persevere as we live a life that imitates Jesus.

COMMENT BOX

█ █ █ █ █ █ █ █ █ █ █ █ █ █ █ █ █ █ █ █

THINK: What went well as you taught this lesson? What can you do better?

_____

_____

_____

_____

_____

_____

_____

_____

TIP: For object lessons from the Old Testament and the life of Jesus, be sure to check out Anne Marie's other books or www.futureflyingsaucers.com.

24 THE LETTERS OF THE NEW TESTAMENT

████████████████████████████████████

Jesus was no longer on earth. The Holy Spirit swept through Jerusalem, causing ordinary disciples to begin doing amazing things for God. Now what? Use everyday mail in this lesson to teach children about the purpose of the Epistles.

Scripture Focus: Romans 1:7; Philippians 1:1-2; James 1:1; 2 Peter 1:1; Revelation 1: 4a

Materials:

- A stack of mail (some advertisements, some bills, and at least one special letter or card from a friend or family member)
- 2 Timothy 3:16-17 poster

Geography: Jerusalem; Judea; Samaria; Rome

Background: The Holy Spirit came as a mighty rushing wind to the disciples. The Old Testament, or Old Covenant, was over. Jesus began the New Covenant. The church age had started, and people were becoming believers by the thousands.

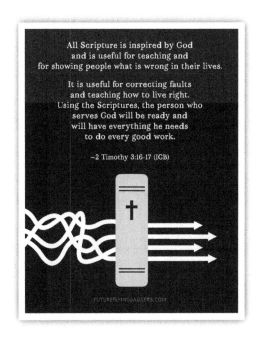

All Scripture is inspired by God and is useful for teaching and for showing people what is wrong in their lives.

It is useful for correcting faults and teaching how to live right. Using the Scriptures, the person who serves God will be ready and will have everything he needs to do every good work.

–2 Timothy 3:16-17 (ICB)

FUTUREFLYINGSAUCERS.COM

OBJECT LESSON

{Hold up the stack of mail and ask:}

- Do you like to go to the mailbox and get the mail? [Allow for answers.]
- What types of things come in the mail? [Letters, advertisements, newspapers, packages, etc.]

{As you go through the types of mail, be dramatic as you describe each one.}

I enjoy receiving mail! It is always so fun to see what I receive!

{Hold up the advertisements.}

These business advertisements are colorful, and at times they can give me interesting information, but these businesses do not love me. They just want me to come into their store or go to their event. In fact, these advertisements are sent to EVERYONE in the town, not just to me. They do not really care about me as a person.

{Ask:}

- Where do most of these advertisements end up? [In the trash]

{Hold up the bills.}

These envelopes hold monthly bills. These are businesses to which I owe money. Each month I have to pay for power, water, the mortgage, and more.

{Ask:}

- Do these businesses care whether or not I pay them? [Yes!]

Yes, they care if I pay them for their services. In fact, if I do not pay them, they can charge me a fee OR even turn off whatever the service is.

{Ask:}

- Do these businesses care about me as a person? Or do they want my money? [They want money for the service they give.]

I am not the only person who pays for water or electricity. They send these bills out to thousands of people. I am just one of many. There is nothing special about these bill envelopes.

{Hold up the personal letter or card.}

THIS envelope is different! This is a special letter that I received from _____. She wrote it in her own hand—no computer. In fact, what she wrote in the letter was encouraging to me, and I kept it to read when I need to be encouraged.

{Ask:}

- Do you like getting letters or emails from friends? [Yes]
- How do you feel when you get a letter? [Allow for answers, such as loved, thought of, special, etc.]

The person who wrote this card did not have to write it. She thought of me and my family when we were not around. She took time out of her busy schedule to sit down and write these words. She thought about what she wrote and was motivated to do something nice for me. All of that makes this one letter extremely special.

After Jesus rose from the dead and ascended into heaven, many of the apostles wrote letters to new believers.

BIBLE LESSON

As Peter, the apostles, and Paul preached, more and more people became a part of The Way. Some leaders stayed in Jerusalem, while others traveled to Judea, Samaria, and other nations.

Those like Paul who traveled to other cities and nations usually went to the Jewish synagogues to preach to the Jews first. Some believed, but most did not. Israel had hardened its heart toward the Lord. Therefore, these first missionaries began to preach to the Gentiles. God had now begun blessing every family in the world as the gospel of salvation spread.

The leaders and teachers could not be at every church they started. Paul would stay a little while and then move on to the next place. He wanted to be sure that the churches were growing in Christ, and he wanted to encourage the church leaders. Therefore, Paul wrote many letters.

Peter and John, the apostles, also wrote letters. God spoke through these men to the people. By reading the letters, new Christians would gain understanding about God. They would be encouraged and receive instructions on how to live a righteous life pleasing unto the Lord. God wants us to allow Him to change our hearts to be more like Jesus. God wants us to glorify Him.

{Read the introduction Scripture verses: Romans 1:7; Philippians 1:1-2; James 1:1; 2 Peter 1:1; Revelation 1:4a. All of these are letter introductions. Ask:}

- What types of words do you hear in these greetings? [Grace and peace to you; bondservant; Jesus; to the saints; beloved of God]

- Are these personal words? [Yes]

- What does that tell you about the men who wrote these letters? [They loved the people to whom they were writing. They cared about what happened to them.]

All of the letters, or epistles, that are written in the New Testament are there for a reason. All of them teach us more about who God is, who Jesus is, and how people should respond to them. Some of the letters give instructions. Other letters are meant to encourage believers during persecution. Some of the letters were written to individuals asking them to do something specific.

One apostle, John, had something very special happen to him. John had been banished to the island of Patmos because he taught about Jesus. While there, the Lord appeared to John and gave him a vision for the future.

John wrote down the vision in the Book of Revelation. In this book there are seven letters to seven churches. These letters help us know what pleases God and what does not. We learn more about Jesus' glory and how He is the King of Kings and Lord of Lords. We also learn about the return of Jesus.

LIFE APPLICATION

{Hold up the personal letter.}

This letter is special. I have read it more than once. I do not throw it away. It has a purpose.

Just like the early church members, we should be reading the letters written by the apostles. We should be learning how to live a life that is pleasing to the Lord.

In a letter that Paul wrote to a man named Timothy, Paul tells Timothy that all Scripture is good for teaching, rebuking, correction, and training in righteousness. Therefore, reading these letters, and all of the Bible, helps us to know what is right (Jesus), to know what we are doing wrong (sin), and to know how to correct our lives so we can be righteous through Jesus (repentance and salvation through faith).

How are you going to know how to love God with all you heart, mind, and soul if you do not read what He has told you?

One of the things John saw in his vision was a book called the Book of Life. Only Jesus is able to open that book. In that book is the name of every person who has accepted Jesus Christ as his or her Savior.

Is your name written in the book?

What can we learn from the letters of the New Testament? God is a personal God, and He wants a relationship with each person He has created. While we were still sinners, Jesus died for us. If we, in faith, believe in Jesus, then we should desire to do all we can, with the guidance of the Holy Spirit, to tell others about Him and live a life worthy of our Holy God.

COMMENT BOX

■ ■ ■ ■ ■ ■ ■ ■ ■ ■ ■ ■ ■ ■ ■ ■ ■ ■ ■ ■

THINK: What went well as you taught this lesson? What can you do better?

_____

_____

_____

_____

_____

_____

_____

_____

_____

TIP: Once children choose to follow Jesus, they need to be taught HOW to follow Jesus. Consider reading the book *Mateo's Choice* or teaching through *Walk This Way: Ethics and Sanctification Lessons for Kids*.

EXTRA RESOURCES

HOW TO LEAD
A CHILD TO CHRIST

■■■■■■■■■■■■■■■■■■■■■■■■■■

After you teach a Bible lesson, there are times when it is necessary to ask the children if they want to follow Jesus through faith. Always have those who want to make some sort of decision leave the larger groups of kids. I do this by either having them stay behind while the others leave, or by taking the small group into another room. I do this because it causes the child to physically make a decision: *"Do I stay? Or not?"* This also allows for fewer distractions. (Always be sure to have another adult nearby. That's a safety rule!)

Ask many questions; you want the children to think through what they are doing. These questions should not be answered by *"Yes," "No,"* or *"Jesus."* Use lots of Scripture, because you want God's Word to be working.

There is no minimum age for salvation. Even three-year-olds can recognize they are sinners and be sorry for what they do. However, you do want to be sure that the child, no matter the age, understands this lifelong commitment to Jesus.

Salvation is a big deal, and you do not want a child to make a decision that is not understood or taken seriously. If at any point you sense that there is confusion or uncertainty on the child's part, say, *"I can tell that God is working in your heart. I want you to keep listening and learning."* Then dismiss that child who is not ready to join the rest of the group.

Examples of Counseling Questions:

- Why have you decided to talk with me?
- Why do you need Jesus as your Savior?
- What is sin?
- What are some examples of sin?
- Can you do anything to get rid of sin?
- Read Romans 3:23.
- Who is Jesus?
- What did Jesus do for you?
- Read 1 Corinthians 15:3-4.
- Read John 3:16 or Acts 16:31.
- Would you like to pray to God and tell Him about your faith in Jesus?

If the child understands the questions and is answering appropriately, describe salvation as a heart change—a desire to live God's way. If the child is serious about dealing with sin and wanting to live for Jesus, explain that he or she needs to talk to God and that talking to God is called prayer.

At this point lead the child in prayer. Have the child copy what you say, or tell the child what information should be included when asking God for salvation:

- Admit to God that you are a sinner.
- Say that you are sorry for those sins. Ask for forgiveness.
- Tell Jesus you believe Jesus is God's Son and that He died on the cross and rose again.
- Confess that Jesus is your Lord and Master.
- Thank God for saving you.

Once the child has prayed, read Hebrews 13:5b and 6a. Ask, *"What has Jesus done for you?"* This will give assurance of salvation.

Pray for that child when you are finished. Then have the child choose at least one person to tell about what happened (usually a parent).

Rejoice with the family!

It is possible you might have a situation that includes parents who are not happy about the choice made by their child. If this happens, explain the decision to the parents, but then, if at all possible, disciple that child yourself. If the child goes to another church or no church at all, check on the child when you can. Definitely pray for that young Christian.

Be sure to tell your pastor of the child's decision so he can follow up with the family and discuss baptism.

If you are a parent and your child has accepted Jesus as his or her Savior, be sure to help your child grow in knowledge and service.

** Consider giving the child a copy of *Mateo's Choice* to help disciple him and share the gospel with his family.

HOW TO BECOME AN EXCELLENT BIBLE TEACHER

■ ■

When teaching children, our goal is two-fold. First, we want kids to **get right** with God through a saving faith. Second, we want our children to **stay right** with God through the sanctification process.

> You, however, continue in the things you have learned and become convinced of, knowing from whom you have learned them, and that from childhood you have known the sacred writings which are able to give you the wisdom that leads to salvation through faith which is in Christ Jesus. All Scripture is inspired by God and profitable for teaching, for reproof, for correction, for training in righteousness; so that the man of God may be adequate, equipped for every good work.
>
> 2 Timothy 3:14-17 (NASB)

WHAT We Want to Teach:

We want to focus on verse 16, because if we can (1) **teach** doctrine in a way that reveals sin, and then (2) explain how to stop sinning (**reproof**), and then (3) counsel children how to fix their sin problems (**correction**), THEN (4) they will be restored to a character of **righteousness** so God can use them for good works. This is the cycle of sanctification after salvation. All of this happens through the power of the Holy Spirit.

However, the cycle of sanctification does not revolve in a circle. It is more like a spiral. As we grow closer to God and He works on our hearts, then we become closer to the center, or place of total perfection. We will not ever reach perfection this side of heaven, but we are on a journey with God to walk on His path of righteousness.

We can also think of it this way: As our view of God increases, our view of ourselves decreases. (Sounds like John the Baptist!) The discrepancy is seen more and more. Jesus becomes bigger in our lives the more we know of Him. He must increase. We must decrease. Yes, we are children of God and heirs to a Kingdom, but we are clothed in unrighteous rags. We need Jesus.

This is what we want for our children, whether they are our own or those we teach in the church. **We want them to view Jesus as being the One and Only Greatest Person in their lives.**

HOW We Teach This:

In order to be an excellent Bible teacher, a person must seek God first and foremost. **I fail at this.** I am not an excellent Bible teacher because of what I do, but because of what God chooses to do through me. I attempt to read the Bible every day. I attempt to make good choices. I mess up.

I think this is what makes the difference between a mediocre Bible teacher and an excellent Bible teacher: **An excellent Bible teacher daily recognizes his or her own need for a Savior**.

It is through our failings that Christ shines His light into our Bible lessons. When we explain to children how God is real, forgiving, and personal in our own lives, they will begin to search for that type of relationship as well.

How do we teach children? By allowing God to teach us. This means we need to take an honest look at ourselves, evaluate our hearts, and apply what God shows us to our teaching.

Prayerfully read through the next few questions and answer them.

Evaluation of Yourself:

1. Are you sold out to Jesus?
2. How enthusiastic are you about your teaching?
3. Are you interested in your children's lives?
4. Can you sense the needs of your children?
5. Are you a servant leader?

Evaluation of Each Bible Lesson:

1. Did you accomplish your objectives?
2. If not, why?
3. What was weak?
4. What was strong?
5. What changes should you make before the next lesson or before you teach this lesson again?

Evaluation of the Teaching Year:

1. How many salvations took place among your children?
2. Can you see a growth of Biblical knowledge in your children?
3. Was there growth in their spiritual heart knowledge?

"To whom would He teach knowledge,
And to whom would He interpret the message?
Those just weaned from milk?
Those just taken from the breast?
"For He says,
'Order on order, order on order,
Line on line, line on line,
A little here, a little there.'"

Isaiah 28:9-10 (NASB)

Biblical knowledge, or learning the Scriptures, takes a lifetime. It involves a little truth here and a little lesson there, step by step. We Bible teachers want our children to discover for themselves what they **ought** to do, so that through loving God, they will **obey** Him regardless of any obstacles. **A committed will to obey God equals a changed life.**

A NOTE FROM THE AUTHOR

■ ■

Friend, I encourage you. You hold the living, powerful Word of God in your hands. Use it wisely. Read it lovingly. Teach from it enthusiastically. Love powerfully. **Be Excellent!!**

Your Servant,

Anne Marie
FutureFlyingSaucers.com

COLORING PAGES

"But the Holy Spirit will come to you. Then you will receive power. You will be my witnesses—in Jerusalem, in all of Judea, in Samaria, and in every part of the world."

–Acts 1:8 (ICB)

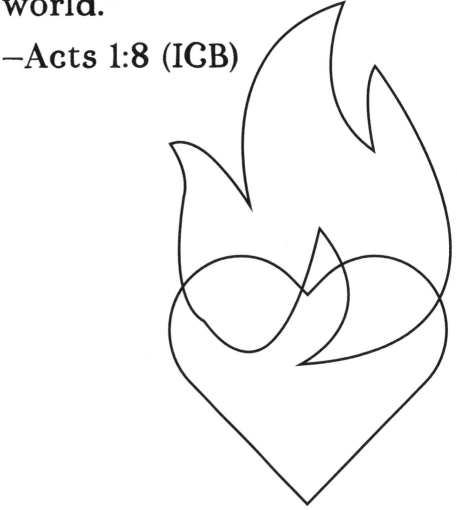

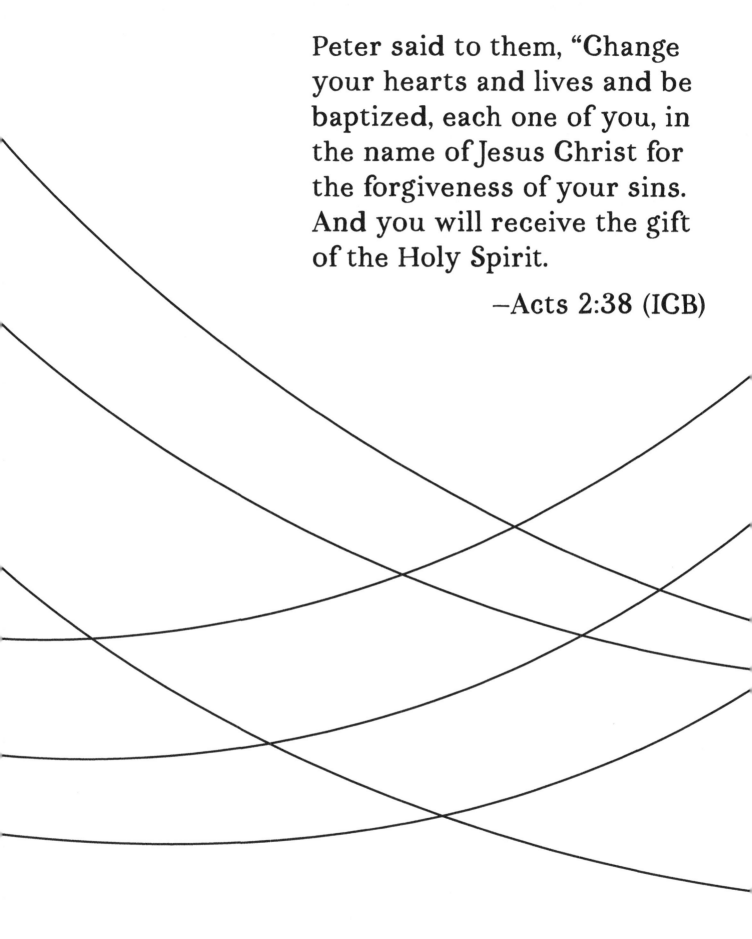

Peter said to them, "Change your hearts and lives and be baptized, each one of you, in the name of Jesus Christ for the forgiveness of your sins. And you will receive the gift of the Holy Spirit.

–Acts 2:38 (ICB)

But Peter said,

"I don't have any silver or gold,
but I do have something else I can give you:
By the power of Jesus Christ from Nazareth
—stand up and walk!"

–Acts 3:8 (ICB)

The whole church
and all the others
who heard about these things
were filled with

FEAR.

–Acts 5:11 (ICB)

The apostles
left the meeting
FULL OF JOY
because they were
given the honor of
suffering disgrace for Jesus.

–Acts 5:41 (ICB)

But Stephen was
full of the Holy Spirit.
He looked up to heaven
and saw the glory of God.
He saw Jesus standing
at God's right side.
He said,

"Look! I see heaven open.
And I see the Son of Man
standing at God's right side!"

−Acts 7:55-56 (ICB)

Then Philip said,

"If you believe with all your heart, you may."

And he answered and said,

"I believe that Jesus Christ is the Son of God."

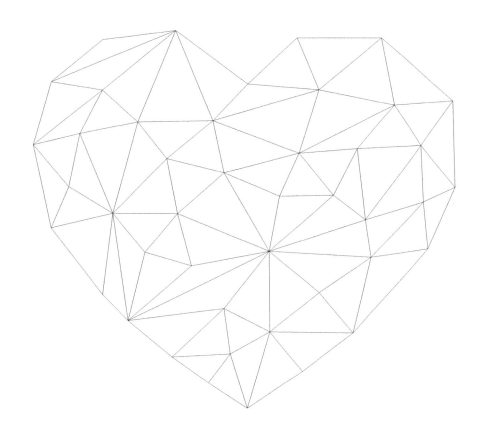

–Acts 8:37 (NKJV)

Peter began to speak:

"I really understand now that to God every person is the same.

God accepts anyone who worships him and does what is right.

It is not important what country a person comes from."

–Acts 10:34-35 (ICB)

Then Peter realized what had happened.

He thought,

"Now I know that the Lord
really sent his angel to me.
He rescued me from Herod and
from all the things the Jewish people
thought would happen."

–Acts 12:11 (ICB)

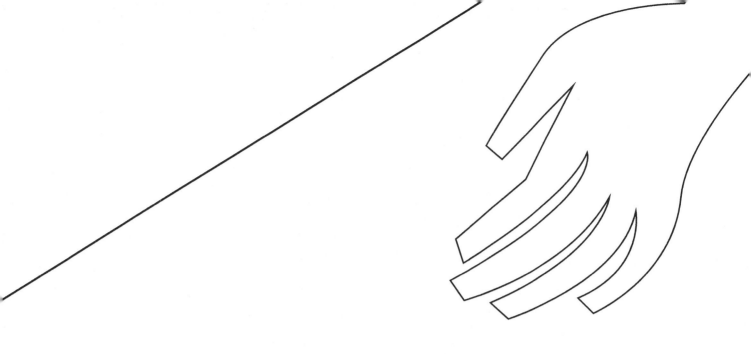

They were all worshiping the Lord
and giving up eating. The Holy Spirit said to them,

"Give Barnabas and Saul
to me to do a special work.
I have chosen them for it."

–Acts 13:2 (ICB)

In those cities they made the
followers of Jesus stronger.
They helped them to stay in the faith.
They said,

"We must suffer many things
to enter God's kingdom."

–Acts 14:22 (ICB)

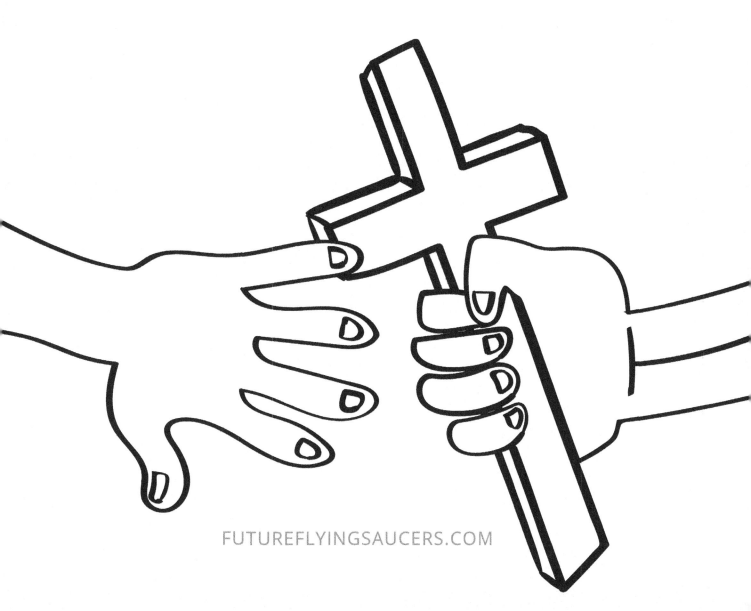

God, who knows the thoughts
of all men, accepted them.
He showed this to us by
giving them the Holy Spirit,
just as he did to us.

–Acts 15:8 (ICB)

They said to him,

"Believe in the Lord Jesus and you will be saved— you and all the people in your house."

–Acts 16:31 (ICB)

These Jews were better
than the Jews in Thessalonica.
They were eager to hear
the things Paul and Silas said.

These Jews in Berea studied the Scriptures
every day to find out if these things were true.

–Acts 17:11 (ICB)

Silas and Timothy came from
Macedonia and joined Paul in Corinth.
After this, Paul used all his time
telling people the Good News.
He showed the Jews that

JESUS IS THE CHRIST.

–Acts 18:5 (ICB)

In a powerful way
the word of the Lord kept
spreading and growing.

–Acts 19:20 (ICB)

But now I must obey the Holy Spirit and go to Jerusalem. I don't know what will happen to me there. I know only that in every city the Holy Spirit tells me that troubles and even jail wait for me.

–Acts 20:22-23
(ICB)

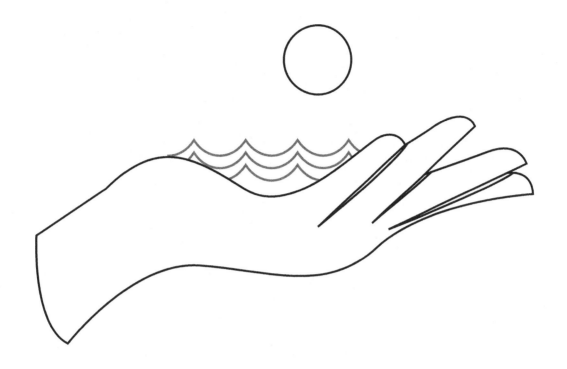

"You will be his witness to all people.
You will tell them about the things you have
seen and heard. Now, why wait any longer?
Get up, be baptized, and wash your sins away.
Do this, trusting in him to save you."

-Acts 22:15-16 (ICB)

The next night the Lord came

and stood by Paul. He said,

"BE BRAVE!
You have told people
in Jerusalem about me.
You must do the same
in Rome also."

–Acts 23:11 (ICB)

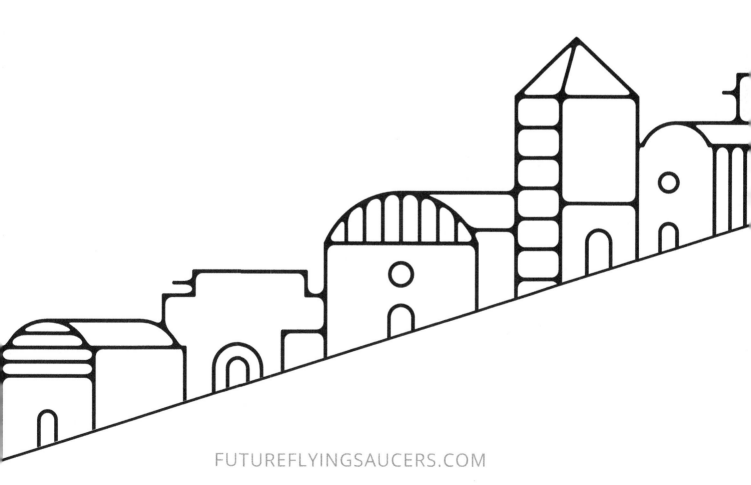

Paul said,

"Whether it is a short or a long time,
I pray to God that not only you but
EVERY PERSON
listening to me today
would be saved and be like me—
except for these
chains I have!"

–Acts 26:29 (ICB)

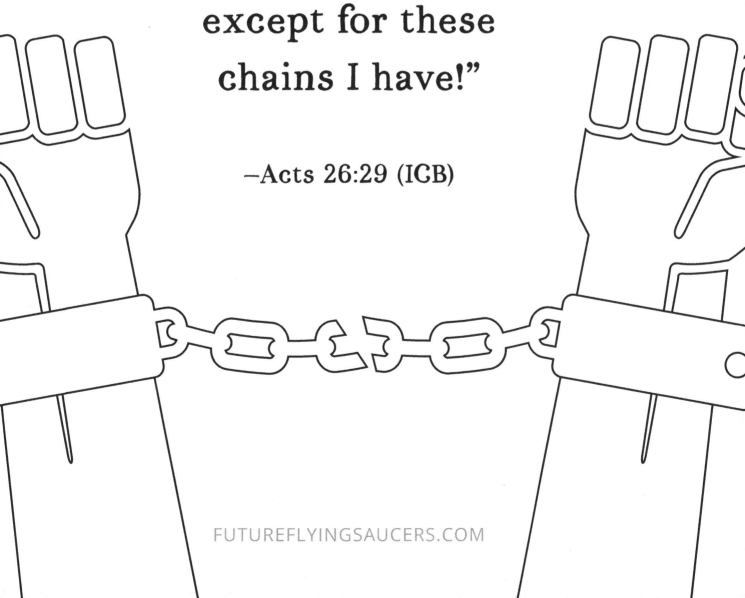

So men, be cheerful!
I trust in God.
Everything will happen
as his angel told me.

–Acts 27:25 (ICB)

"I want you Jews to know
that God has also sent his salvation
to the non-Jewish people.
They will listen!"

–Acts 28:28 (ICB)

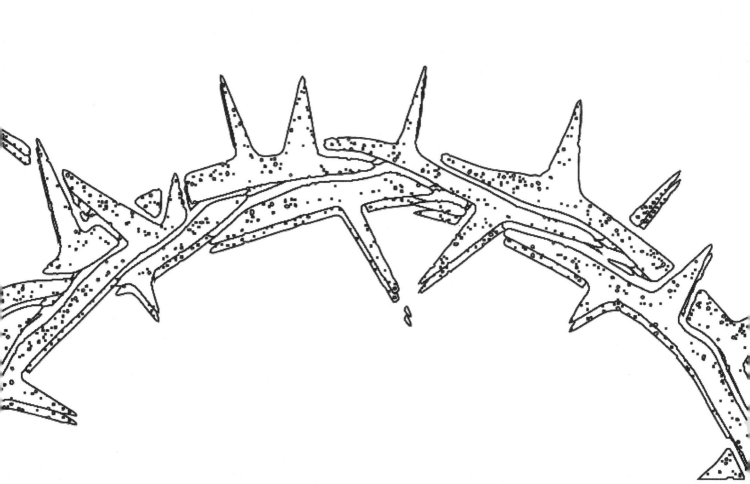

All Scripture is inspired by God
and is useful for teaching and
for showing people what is wrong in their lives.

It is useful for correcting faults
and teaching how to live right.
Using the Scriptures, the person who
serves God will be ready and
will have everything he needs
to do every good work.

–2 Timothy 3:16-17 (ICB)

Made in the USA
Middletown, DE
25 February 2022

61839064R00137